KU-468-648

Collins

175 YEARS OF DICTIONARY PUBLISHING

easy learning
English
Spelling

Collins

HarperCollins Publishers
Westerhill Road
Bishopbriggs
Glasgow
G64 2QT

First edition 2010

Reprint 3

© HarperCollins Publishers 2010

ISBN 978-0-00-734117-7

Collins ® is a registered trademark of
HarperCollins Publishers Limited

www.collinslanguage.com

A catalogue record for this book is
available from the British Library

Typeset by Davidson Publishing
Solutions, Glasgow

Printed in Great Britain by Clays Ltd,
St Ives plc

Editorial staff

Written by: Ian Brookes

Editor: Lisa Sutherland

For the publisher:
Lucy Cooper
Kerry Ferguson
Elaine Higgleton

introduction

Collins Easy Learning English Spelling is suitable for everyone who wants to know more about spelling and who wants to write more accurately and impressively. The book uses simple explanations, backed up with examples demonstrating each point, to describe the important features of English spelling. It also points out the most difficult words to spell and offers ways of learning these.

The book begins with a clear explanation of how the letters and groups of letters regularly correspond to certain sounds, and then looks at the reasons why the spelling of some words does not match the sound. Next, it looks at recurring patterns and rules with which you need to be familiar to understand and predict how the majority of words are spelt. The last part of the book is concerned with words whose spellings are not easy to predict: it provides some practical advice on learning tricky spellings and then looks at tricky words themselves, showing why each can present pitfalls even to experienced users of English.

All of the hard words that are examined in this book are listed in an alphabetical index at the end of the book. You can use this index both as a resource for checking the correct spellings of tricky words and also to point you to the book's explanations and useful tips for memorizing many of the words.

English spelling can sometimes appear to be a chaotic affair, with the spellings of words such as *choir*, *colonel*, *laugh*, and *yacht* having little relation to the way that words are pronounced in spoken English. Yet there are rules and patterns at work in the spelling system, and it is possible to become a good speller by mastering relatively few of these simple rules and patterns. *Collins Easy Learning English Spelling* is designed to help you with this task, and is a valuable resource for all users of English.

Ian Brookes, 2010

contents

the basics of spelling

The basics of spelling

Spelling is the process of using letters to represent a word. For most words there is one arrangement of letters that is accepted as the correct spelling. Using the correct spelling of a word means that you can be confident of being understood when you write English; getting the spelling wrong can make it difficult to be understood and create a bad impression.

The alphabet

There are twenty-six letters that are used to spell words in English:

a b c d e f g h i j k l m n o p q r s t u v w x y z

Each of these letters can also be written as a capital letter. This form is used at the beginning of a sentence or a name, and in certain other places (see page 77–78).

A B C D E F G H I J K L M N O P Q R S T U V W X Y Z

Five of these letters (**A**, **E**, **I**, **O**, **U**) are **vowels**. These are used to represent sounds that are made when your mouth is open.

cat	*pen*	*sit*
dog	*cup*	

The other letters are called **consonants**. These are used to represent sounds that are made by closing your mouth or using your tongue.

pea	*see*	*do*

> The letter **Y** can act as a vowel in some words, such as *sky* and *crypt*.

Most words are spelt using a mixture of vowels and consonants. This is because in most cases we need to open our mouths between pronouncing different consonants. It is unusual to find more than two vowels or two consonants together.

Typical letter-sounds

Most consonants are strongly associated with a particular sound and represent this sound in virtually every word in which they appear. For example, the letter **B** nearly always makes the same sound.

big	*bad*	*bee*
cab	*club*	*robin*

Some consonants can represent different sounds in different words. For example **C** can have a 'hard' sound like a **K**.

cat	*cup*	*panic*

But it can also have a 'soft' sound like an **S**.

city	*acid*	*place*

Combinations of consonants

Some consonants can be combined and still keep their typical sounds. The letters **L**, **R** and **W** can come after some other consonants.

blob	*grip*	*dwell*
clip	*prod*	*twin*

The letter **S** can come before a number of other consonants.

scan	**sk**ip	**sl**ip
smell	**sn**ip	**sp**in
squid	**st**op	**sw**im

Some combinations of letters can appear in the middle of a word or at the end of a word, but not at the start of a word.

do**ct**or	le**ft**	**gold**en
mi**lk**	he**lp**	be**lt**
la**mp**	la**nd**	ri**ng**
ta**nk**	we**nt**	o**pt**

It is unusual, but not impossible, to have three consonants together.

scrap	**spl**it	ex**tr**a

Combinations that produce typical sounds

When some letters are combined with an **H**, they do not keep their own sounds but create a different sound. For example:

CH

chip	**ch**at	ri**ch**

PH creates the same sound as the letter **F**.

phone	**ph**antom	gra**ph**

SH

ship	**sh**op	fi**sh**

TH

thin   thank   path

TH can also make a different, slightly softer sound.

this   that   with

Simple vowel sounds

The vowels **A**, **E**, **I**, **O**, and **U** each have typical sounds when they appear on their own in short words.

cat	rat	hat
men	pen	ten
bit	hit	sit
dot	lot	got
but	nut	hut

The sound of a vowel changes from a 'short' sound to a 'long' sound when the consonant after the vowel is followed by the letter **E**.

date	rate	hate
scene	swede	theme
bite	mite	like
note	lone	mole
flute	rule	brute

Combinations of vowels

When two vowels are used together, they usually make a different sound rather than keeping the simple sounds they make on their own.

The letters **AI** have a characteristic sound when they appear together.

> *raid* *train* *aim*

The letters **AU** have a characteristic sound when they appear together.

> *daub* *faun* *haul*

The letters **EA** have a characteristic sound when they appear together.

> *read* *tea* *eat*

When the letter **E** is doubled it produces a characteristic sound.
The sound is the same as the one typically produced by **EA**.

> *feed* *tree* *bee*

The letters **IE** have a characteristic sound when they appear together.

> *tie* *fried* *pie*

The letters **OA** have a characteristic sound when they appear together.

> *road* *goat* *toad*

The letters **OE** have a characteristic sound when they appear together.
The sound is the same as the one typically produced by **OA**.

> *toe* *hoe* *woe*

The letters **OI** have a characteristic sound when they appear together.

> *coin* *soil* *oil*

When the letter **O** is doubled it produces a characteristic sound.

> *food* *moon* *boot*

The double **O** can sometimes make a different, shorter, sound.

good   *wool*   *hood*

The letters **OU** have a characteristic sound when they appear together.

mouth   *count*   *out*

The letters **UE** have a characteristic sound when they appear together. The sound is the same as the one produced by **OO** in the word *book*.

true   *sue*   *glue*

Vowels followed by R, W, or Y

When the letters **R**, **W**, or **Y** come after a vowel, the letter usually changes the sound of the vowel, but it is not sounded itself.

The letters **AR** have a characteristic sound when they appear together.

car   *park*   *art*

The letters **AW** have a characteristic sound when they appear together. The sound is the same as the one typically produced by **AU**.

paw   *claw*   *straw*

The letters **AY** have a characteristic sound when they appear together. The sound is the same as the one typically produced by **AI**.

day   *stay*   *may*

The letters **ER** have a characteristic sound when they appear together.

her   *term*   *herb*

The letters **EW** have a characteristic sound when they appear together. The sound is the same as the one produced by **OO** in the word *book*.

flew   *yew*   *brew*

The letters **IR** have a characteristic sound when they appear together. The sound is the same as the one typically produced by **ER**.

sir   *girl*   *shirt*

The letters **OR** have a characteristic sound when they appear together. The sound is the same as the one typically produced by **AU**.

sort   *born*   *for*

The letters **OW** have a characteristic sound when they appear together. The sound is the same as the one typically produced by **OU**.

how   *growl*   *down*

These letters can also make the sound that is typically produced by **OE**.

grow   *flow*   *own*

The letters **OY** have a characteristic sound when they appear together. The sound is the same as the one typically produced by **OI**.

boy   *toy*   *joy*

The letters **UR** have a characteristic sound when they appear together. The sound is the same as the one typically produced by **ER**.

burn   *turn*   *hurt*

why you need to work at spelling

Why you need to work at spelling

If every letter represented one sound and one sound only, you could write out words very easily once you knew which letter represented which sound. Some languages (such as Italian) are indeed quite like this, and present few surprises with regard to spelling once you know how each sound is written.

But English uses about 44 different sounds to make up words, whereas there are only 26 letters to indicate these sounds. This means that some letters have to be used for more than one sound.

Moreover, there are certain other factors that mean that it is not always easy to predict how an English word will be spelt. We shall look at these factors in this chapter.

Some letters can have more than one sound

As we have just seen, there are more sounds in English than there are letters to represent them. This means that some letters have to represent more than sound.

For example, the letter **T** usually makes one sound when it occurs on its own.

    *t*in   *t*ank   pa*t*

But it makes a different sound when it is followed by **H**.

    *th*in   *th*ank   pa*th*

More awkwardly, some letters have more than one sound, even though there are other letters which make one of the sounds. For example, the letter **G** typically has a 'hard' sound when it occurs on its own.

    girl   *game*   *rug*

But in some cases it makes the same 'soft' sound as the letter **J**.

    germ   *ginger*   *page*

Similarly, the letter **S** has a characteristic 'hissing' sound.

    see   *sit*   *gas*

But it can sometimes make the same 'buzzing' sound as the letter **Z**.

    has   *his*   *pleasant*

The fact that letters can have multiple uses means that when you see a word you cannot automatically know how it will be pronounced.

Some sounds can be represented by different letters

A more significant issue is that some sounds can be represented by different letters or combinations of letters.

The vowel sound in the following group of words has the same pronunciation, but the letters used to represent the sound are different in each word.

    march   *alms*   *clerk*   *heart*

The same thing can be true of most vowel sounds, as the following groups of words show.

*ai*sle	*guy*	m*igh*t	*rye*
p*ai*d	d*ay*	gr*ey*	n*eigh*
b*ear*	d*are*	st*air*	wh*ere*
z*oo*	d*o*	sh*oe*	y*ou*

Similarly, the consonant sound at the end of the following words has the same pronunciation, but is represented by different letters in each word.

i*f*	gra*ph*	rou*gh*

The same thing can be true of other consonant sounds, as the following groups of words show.

*g*em	e*dge*	*j*am
*c*ap	*d*ark	pla*que*
*s*it	*c*entre	*sc*ene

So when you hear a word, you can't automatically work out how it is spelt.

Some words that sound the same are written differently

Because sounds can be represented by different letters, it is possible for two different words to sound the same but be spelt differently. This can lead to confusion between the two spellings.

For example, the words *there*, meaning 'that place', and *their*, meaning 'belonging to them' both have the same sound. Similarly, the words *stare*, meaning 'to look intently', and *stair*, meaning 'one of a set of steps', also share a single pronunciation.

It can be easy to confuse these words and use the correct spelling of one word when you are actually intending to write the other word.

English words come from many different languages

One of the most striking features of the English language is its readiness to accept words from other languages. At the heart of modern English are two completely different languages – Anglo-Saxon and French – which have two different spelling systems, but which both contributed thousands of words to the language. In addition to this, English has borrowed words from many other European languages, such as Italian, Spanish, German, and Dutch. Furthermore, whenever scientists made new discoveries they turned to the classical languages of Latin and Greek to come up with names for the new things they needed to describe.

As communications between different parts of the world have become easier, more and more languages have contributed to English, including Turkish, Arabic, Hindi, Chinese, Japanese, and Urdu.

Each of these languages has its own spelling system – many of which are quite different from the natural English system – and the words that English has borrowed from them often keep the spelling patterns of the original language.

For example, many words that come from French use **CH** where you might expect **SH**.

*ch*alet   *ch*ute   *ch*auffeur

Words that come from Greek use **PH** rather than **F**.

tele*ph*one   *ph*ysical   *ph*otograph

Words that come from Japanese use **K** rather than **C**.

karaoke   *karate*   *kimono*

So unless you know which language a word comes from, the spelling could reflect any of a number of different systems.

Silent letters

Another thing that can be confusing is that some words contain letters which are not sounded when the word is pronounced.

Often these are letters that were sounded in the original form of a word. Over many years the pronunciation of these words became simplified, but the spelling has not changed to reflect the new pronunciation.

For example, the letter **G** is often silent before **N** or **M**.

gnat   *phlegm*   *sign*

Similarly, **H** is often silent at the start of a word, or after **G** or **R**.

honest   *ghost*   *rhyme*

E is often silent at the end of words.

have   *give*   *love*

> In fact, it has been reckoned that of the 26 letters in the alphabet, only five are never silent. These five are **F**, **J**, **Q**, **V** and **X**.

The presence of single and double letters

All of the letters except **H**, **Q** and **Y** can occur as both single and double letters within a word.

For example, the letter **B** occurs as a single letter in some words.

    *ro**b**in*   *ha**b**it*   *cra**b***

But in other words the **B** is doubled.

    *bo**bb**in*   *ra**bb**it*   *e**bb***

When consonants are doubled, they are pronounced just the same as a single consonant. So when you hear a word you cannot always tell where a consonant sound is represented by a single letter or a double letter.

Spelling variants

Some words do not have a single spelling that is regarded as correct, but can be spelt in two or more different ways.

For example, most words that end in **ISE** can also end in **IZE** in British English.

specialise   *specialize*
emphasise   *emphasize*

Some words that come from other languages can be written in different ways in English because the original language uses a different alphabet and there are different systems for representing that alphabet in English.

veranda   *verandah*
czar   *tsar*

Other spelling variations are simply a matter of taste.

barbecue   *barbeque*
judgment   *judgement*

The fact that such variations exist means that there is not always a single correct spelling that you can learn.

American and British spelling

One of the most common sources of variations in spelling is the fact that some words are conventionally spelt differently in American English and British English. Some spellings that are regarded as correct by American speakers are not used in Britain (or in Australia and most other English-speaking countries).

The table below shows some examples of variations between British and American spelling.

British English	American English
aesthetic	*esthetic*
aluminium	*aluminum*
anaesthetic	*anesthetic*
analyse	*analyze*
axe	*ax*
behaviour	*behavior*
breathalyse	*breathalyze*
catalogue	*catalog*
centre	*center*
cheque	*check*
colour	*color*
defence	*defense*
favourite	*favorite*
fulfil	*fulfill*
grey	*gray*
instalment	*installment*
jewellery	*jewelry*
kerb	*curb*
litre	*liter*
lustre	*luster*
meagre	*meager*
mould	*mold*

British English	American English
moustache	mustache
odour	odor
plough	plow
programme	program
pyjamas	pajamas
sceptic	skeptic
theatre	theater
tyre	tire
vice	vise
[=woodwork tool]	

And now the good news

All of these factors mean that English spelling needs some work before you can become very accurate. The good news, however, is that there are things you can do to help you understand the system better and so become confident about how to spell words. We shall look at these in the next two chapters.

patterns and building blocks

Patterns and building blocks

Some groups of letters crop up in lots of different English words. Often a group of letters will indicate the same thing in every word that it appears. For example, the letters **RE** at the start of a word usually mean 'again'.

Because so many words are made up of these building blocks, you don't need to learn every spelling individually. Often you can spell out a word by adding together the blocks of letters that form the word. So it is important to know what these blocks are, how they are joined on to the rest of a word, and what they mean.

Building blocks at the start of words

A block of letters that regularly appears at the start of words and carries a meaning is called a **prefix**. A prefix can be fixed in front of another word or block of letters to create a new word with a different meaning.

For example, when the letters **UN** are added to another word (called a **root word**), they add the meaning of 'not' to the sense of the other word.

    ***un**natural*   ***un**known*   ***un**holy*

Notice that you can spell these words by splitting them into the prefix and the root word, as the spelling of the root word stays the same.

It is not always quite as obvious as this that a prefix is being added to an existing word to make a new word. Many prefixes occur in words that came to English from Latin and Greek. In these cases the blocks to which they are joined are often Latin or Greek forms rather than familiar English words. Nevertheless, it is worth studying these building blocks and noting that they occur in many English words.

The prefix **AB** means 'away from' or 'not'.

*ab*normal *ab*use *ab*scond

The prefix **AD** means 'towards'.

*ad*dress *ad*just *ad*mit

The prefix **AL** means 'all'.

*al*together *al*ways *al*mighty

The prefix **ANTE** means 'before'. Take care not to confuse this with **ANTI**. If you remember the meaning of both these prefixes you should be able to work out the correct spelling of a word that starts with one of them.

*ante*natal *ante*room *ante*cedent

The prefix **ANTI** means 'against'. Take care not to confuse this with **ANTE**. If you remember the meaning of both these prefixes you should be able to work out the correct spelling of a word that starts with one of them.

*anti*war *anti*social *anti*depressant

The prefix **ARCH** means 'chief'.

*arch*bishop *arch*enemy *arch*angel

The prefix **AUTO** means 'self'.

*auto*graph *auto*biography *auto*mobile

The prefix **BENE** means 'good' or 'well'.

*bene*fit *bene*volent *bene*factor

The prefix **BI** means 'two' or 'twice'.

      bicycle   *bimonthly*   *bifocals*

The prefix **CIRCUM** means 'around'.

      circumference   *circumstance*   *circumnavigate*

The prefix **CO** means 'together'. There is sometimes a hyphen after this prefix to make the meaning clear.

      copilot   *co*-star   *cooperate*

The prefix **CON** means 'together'.

      confer   *constellation*   *converge*

When it is added before words beginning with **L**, the prefix **CON** is changed to **COL**.

      collaborate   *collateral*   *collide*

When it is added before words beginning with **B**, **M**, or **P**, the prefix **CON** is changed to **COM**.

      combat   *commit*   *compact*

When it is added before words beginning with **R**, the prefix **CON** is changed to **COR**.

      correct   *correspond*   *correlation*

The prefix **CONTRA** means 'against'.

      contradict   *contravene*   *contraflow*

The prefix **DE** indicates removal or reversal.

*de*frost   *de*throne   *de*caffeinated

The prefix **DIS** indicates removal or reversal.

*dis*agree   *dis*honest   *dis*trust

The prefix **EN** usually means 'into'.

*en*rage   *en*slave   *en*danger

The prefix **EX** means 'out' or 'outside of'.

*ex*it   *ex*port   *ex*ternal

The prefix **EX** also means 'former'. The prefix is followed by a hyphen when it has this meaning.

ex-wife   *ex*-partner   *ex*-president

The prefix **EXTRA** means 'beyond' or 'outside of'.

*extra*ordinary   *extra*terrestrial   *extra*sensory

The prefix **HYPER** means 'over' or 'more'.

*hyper*active   *hyper*critical   *hyper*market

The prefix **IN** sometimes means 'not'.

*in*human   *in*sufferable   *in*credible

The prefix **IN** can also mean 'in' or 'into'.

*in*filtrate   *in*take   *in*grown

When it is added before words beginning with **L**, the prefix **IN** is changed to **IL**.

*ill*iterate *ill*egal *ill*ogical

When it is added before words beginning with **B**, **M**, or **P**, the prefix **IN** is changed to **IM**.

*im*balance *im*moral *im*possible

> Note that the word *input* is an exception to this rule.

When it is added before words beginning with **R**, the prefix **IN** is changed to **IR**.

*irr*egular *irr*esponsible *irr*elevant

The prefix **INTER** means 'between'.

*inter*national *inter*war *inter*ruption

The prefix **INTRA** means 'within'.

*intra*venous *intra*net *intra*mural

The prefix **MACRO** means 'very large'.

*macro*economics *macro*biotic *macro*cosm

The prefix **MAL** means 'bad' or 'badly'.

*mal*practice *mal*formed *mal*administration

The prefix **MAXI** means 'big' or 'biggest'.

*maxi*mize *maxi*mum *maxi*dress

The prefix **MICRO** means 'very small'.

    *micro*scope   *micro*chip   *micro*wave

The prefix **MINI** means 'small'.

    *mini*skirt   *mini*series   *mini*bus

The prefix **MIS** means 'wrong' or 'false'.

    *mis*behave   *mis*fortune   *mis*take

The prefix **NON** means 'not'.

    *non*sense   *non*fiction   *non*stop

The prefix **PARA** usually means 'beside' or 'parallel to'.

    *para*medic   *para*military   *para*legal

The prefix **POST** means 'after'.

    *post*pone   *post*graduate   *post*dated

The prefix **PRE** means 'before'.

    *pre*arranged   *pre*war   *pre*season

The prefix **PRO** means 'ahead' or 'forward'.

    *pro*logue   *pro*active   *pro*voke

The prefix **PRO** also means 'in favour of'. The prefix is followed by a hyphen when it has this meaning.

    pro-choice   *pro*-democracy   *pro*-European

The prefix **RE** means 'again'.

    *re*arrange   *re*read   *re*heat

The prefix **SEMI** means 'half'.

    semi-final   *semi*tone   *semi*-professional

The prefix **SUB** means 'under'.

    *sub*marine   *sub*soil   *sub*way

The prefix **SUPER** indicates 'above', 'beyond' or 'extreme'.

    *super*human   *super*market   *super*star

The prefix **TELE** means 'distant'.

    *tele*graph   *tele*vision   *tele*scope

The prefix **TRANS** means 'across'.

    *trans*fer   *trans*plant   *trans*continental

The prefix **ULTRA** indicates 'beyond' or 'extreme'.

    *ultra*sound   *ultra*modern   *ultra*-careful

Building blocks at the end of words

A block of letters that regularly appears at the end of words and carries a meaning is called a **suffix**. Just like a prefix at the start of a word, a suffix can be fixed onto a root word to create a new word with a different meaning.

For example, when the letters **LESS** are added to the end of a root word, they add the meaning of 'without' to the sense of the root word.

*head**less***   *child**less***   *life**less***

It is worth studying these building blocks and noting that they occur at the end of many English words.

The suffix **ABLE** means 'able to'.

*break**able***   *read**able***   *enjoy**able***

> It is difficult to distinguish this from the suffix **IBLE**, which occurs in many words and has the same meaning. A list of the common words with each suffix is given on pages 33–34.

The suffix **AL** means 'related to'.

*season**al***   *nation**al***   *tradition**al***

The suffix **ANCE** indicates a state or quality.

*accept**ance***   *defi**ance***   *resembl**ance***

The suffix **ANT** indicates an action or condition.

*resist**ant***   *toler**ant***   *dorm**ant***

> It is difficult to distinguish this from the suffix **ENT**, which occurs in many words and has the same meaning. A list of the common words with each suffix is given on pages 35–36.

The suffix **ARY** means 'related to'.

*caution**ary***   *revolution**ary***   *document**ary***

The suffix **ATE** creates verbs indicating becoming or taking on a state.

     hyphenate   *elevate*   *medicate*

The suffix **ATION** indicates becoming or entering a state.

     hyphenation   *elevation*   *medication*

The suffix **CRACY** means 'government'.

     democracy   *autocracy*   *bureaucracy*

The suffix **CRAT** means 'ruler'.

     democrat   *autocrat*   *bureaucrat*

The suffix **DOM** means 'state of being'.

     freedom   *boredom*   *martyrdom*

The suffix **EE** indicates a person who is affected by or receives something.

     interviewee   *evacuee*   *honouree*

The suffix **EN** means 'become'.

     dampen   *deaden*   *blacken*

The suffix **ENCE** indicates a state or quality.

     residence   *abstinence*   *dependence*

The suffix **ENT** indicates an action or condition.

     abstinent   *resident*   *independent*

> It is difficult to distinguish this from the suffix **ANT**, which occurs in many words and has the same meaning. A list of the common words with each suffix is given on pages 35–36.

The suffix **ER** means 'person from'.

*villag**er***	*North**er**ner*	*London**er***

The suffix **ER** also means 'person who does a job' or 'thing that does a job'.

*driv**er***	*paint**er***	*teach**er***
*fasten**er***	*scrap**er***	*light**er***

The suffix **ESCENT** means 'becoming'.

*adol**escent***	*obsol**escent***	*lumin**escent***

The suffix **ETTE** means 'small'.

*kitchen**ette***	*cigar**ette***	*disk**ette***

The suffix **FUL** means 'full of'.

*beauti**ful***	*pain**ful***	*resent**ful***

The suffix **HOOD** means 'state of being'.

*child**hood***	*likeli**hood***	*priest**hood***

The suffix **IAN** creates nouns indicating a member of a profession.

*politic**ian***	*magic**ian***	*mathematic**ian***

The suffix **IBLE** means 'able to'.

> *edible*   *terrible*   *possible*

> It is difficult to distinguish this from the suffix **ABLE**, which occurs in many words and has the same meaning. A list of the common words with each suffix is given on pages 33–34.

The suffix **IC** means 'related to'.

> *atomic*   *periodic*   *rhythmic*

The suffix **IFICATION** creates nouns indicating an action.

> *notification*   *classification*   *clarification*

The suffix **IFY** creates verbs indicating an action.

> *notify*   *classify*   *clarify*

The suffix **ISH** means 'fairly' or 'rather'.

> *smallish*   *youngish*   *brownish*

The suffix **ISH** also means 'resembling'.

> *tigerish*   *boyish*   *amateurish*

The suffix **ISM** means 'action' or 'condition'.

> *criticism*   *heroism*   *absenteeism*

The suffix **ISM** also creates nouns indicating a prejudice.

> *sexism*   *racism*   *anti-Semitism*

The suffix **IST** means 'doer of'.

      motorist   *soloist*   *artist*

The suffix **IST** also indicates a prejudice.

      sexist   *racist*   *ageist*

The suffix **ITY** indicates a state or condition.

      reality   *stupidity*   *continuity*

The suffix **IVE** indicates a tendency towards something.

      explosive   *active*   *decorative*

The suffix **IZE** creates verbs indicating a change or becoming.
Words that end with **IZE** can also be spelt **ISE** in British English.

      radicalize   *legalize*   *economize*
      radicalise   *legalise*   *economise*

The suffix **LET** means 'little'.

      booklet   *ringlet*   *piglet*

The suffix **LIKE** means 'resembling'.

      doglike   *childlike*   *dreamlike*

The suffix **LING** means 'small'.

      duckling   *gosling*   *princeling*

The suffix **LY** means 'in this manner'.

      kindly   *friendly*   *properly*

The suffix **MENT** means 'state of'.

contentment   enjoyment   employment

The suffix **METER** means 'measure'.

thermometer   barometer   speedometer

The suffix **NESS** means 'state of' or 'quality of'.

kindness   blindness   selfishness

The suffix **OLOGY** means 'study of' or 'science of'.

biology   sociology   musicology

The suffix **SHIP** means 'state of' or 'condition of'.

fellowship   dictatorship   horsemanship

The suffix **SION** means 'action' or 'state of'.

confusion   decision   explosion

> It is difficult to distinguish this from the suffix **TION**,
> which occurs in many words and has the same meaning.
> A list of the common words with each suffix is given on
> pages 36–38.

The suffix **SOME** means 'tending to'.

quarrelsome   troublesome   loathsome

The suffix **TION** means 'action' or 'state of'.

creation   production   calculation

> It is difficult to distinguish this from the suffix **TION**, which occurs in many words and has the same meaning. A list of the common words with each suffix is given on pages 36–38.

The suffix **Y** means 'like' or 'full of'.

watery   *hilly*   *snowy*

ABLE and IBLE

The suffixes **ABLE** and **IBLE** are both quite common (although **ABLE** is more common) and have the same meaning. You should be aware of the possibility of confusing these endings and check if you are not sure which one is correct.

The table below shows some common words with each ending.

Words that end in ABLE	Words that end in IBLE
adaptable	accessible
admirable	audible
adorable	credible
advisable	divisible
agreeable	eligible
allowable	flexible
arguable	gullible
available	horrible
capable	illegible
desirable	inaudible
durable	indelible
enjoyable	inedible

Words that end in ABLE	Words that end in IBLE
enviable	invisible
excitable	irresistible
flammable	legible
irritable	negligible
lovable	plausible
movable	possible
notable	risible
palatable	sensible
probable	tangible
suitable	terrible
tolerable	visible

A useful – but not one-hundred per cent reliable – rule of thumb is that when one of these endings is added to an existing word, the spelling is **ABLE**.

adapt**able**   enjoy**able**   lov**able**

Adjectives ending in **ABLE** will form related nouns ending in **ABILITY**.

cap**able**   prob**able**   suit**able**
cap**ability**   prob**ability**   suit**ability**

However, adjectives ending **IBLE** will form related nouns ending in **IBILITY**.

gull**ible**   flex**ible**   poss**ible**
gull**ibility**   flex**ibility**   poss**ibility**

ANT and ENT

The suffixes **ANT** and **ENT** are both quite common and have the same meaning. You should be aware of the possibility of confusing these endings and check if you are not sure which one is correct.

The table below shows some common words with each ending.

Words that end in ANT	Words that end in ENT
abundant	absent
adamant	accident
arrogant	adjacent
assistant	affluent
blatant	ailment
brilliant	ancient
buoyant	apparent
defiant	argument
deodorant	coherent
dominant	deficient
dormant	dependent
elegant	descent
emigrant	efficient
exuberant	eminent
fragrant	equipment
hesitant	evident
ignorant	fluent
immigrant	implement
important	lenient
incessant	negligent
indignant	nutrient
irritant	opulent
migrant	parent
militant	patient
mutant	permanent

Words that end in ANT	Words that end in ENT
occupant	precedent
pleasant	president
poignant	prominent
radiant	pungent
redundant	rodent
relevant	salient
reluctant	silent
stagnant	solvent
tenant	strident
tolerant	succulent
vacant	sufficient
valiant	turbulent

Words ending in **ANT** will form related nouns ending in **ANCE** or **ANCY**.

defi**ant**	tole**rant**	va**cant**
defi**ance**	tole**rance**	va**cancy**

However, words ending **ENT** will form related nouns ending in **ENCE** or **ENCY**.

flu**ent**	opul**ent**	suffici**ent**
flu**ency**	opul**ence**	suffici**ency**

SION and TION

The suffixes **SION** and **TION** are both quite common and have the same meaning (although **TION** is more common). You should be aware of the possibility of confusing these endings and check if you are not sure which one is correct.

The table below shows some common words with each ending.

Words that end in SION	Words that end in TION
adhesion	accusation
admission	ambition
cohesion	assumption
collision	attention
conclusion	audition
confusion	caution
conversion	collection
decision	condition
dimension	congestion
discussion	decoration
division	direction
erosion	duration
evasion	emotion
exclusion	equation
excursion	evolution
expansion	exception
explosion	fiction
illusion	intention
inclusion	invention
invasion	isolation
mansion	location
mission	mention
occasion	motion
omission	nation
permission	nutrition
persuasion	option
possession	pollution
revision	relation
session	separation
television	solution
tension	tuition
version	vacation

Words ending in **SION** are often related to adjectives ending in **SIVE**.

expan**sion**	persua**sion**	permis**sion**
expan**sive**	persua**sive**	permis**sive**

However, words ending **TION** are often related to adjectives ending in **TIVE**.

na**tion**	rela**tion**	atten**tion**
na**tive**	rela**tive**	atten**tive**

Building blocks at the end of verbs

There is a small group of suffixes called **inflections** that are regularly added to the basic forms of verbs. These endings indicate either the time of action or the person performing the action.

The ending **S** is added to verbs to create what is called the **third person singular** form of the present tense – that is, the form used after 'he', 'she', 'it' or a named person or thing when talking about present action.

cheat**s**	cook**s**	walk**s**

The ending **ING** is added to verbs to create the **present participle**, which is used to refer to present action.

cheat**ing**	cook**ing**	walk**ing**

The ending **ED** is added to most verbs to create the **past tense** and **past participle** – forms which are used when talking about action in the past.

cheat**ed**	cook**ed**	walk**ed**

Note that some common verbs have past tenses and past participles which do not end in **ED** but which are formed in an irregular way.

bent	*spent*	*did*
gone	*done*	*fallen*

Building blocks at the end of adjectives

There are two inflection suffixes that are regularly added to the basic forms of adjectives to indicate the degree of the quality indicated by the word.

The ending **ER** is added at the end of an adjective to mean 'more'. This is called the **comparative** form.

*clever**er***	*green**er***	*calm**er***

The ending **EST** is added at the end of an adjective to mean 'most'. This is called the **superlative** form.

*clever**est***	*green**est***	*calm**est***

Note that these suffixes are generally only added to words of one or two syllables. For adjectives with more than two syllables (and some adjectives with two syllables) the most comparative and superlative forms are created by using the words 'more' and 'most'.

more *beautiful*	**more** *interesting*	**more** *loyal*
most *beautiful*	**most** *interesting*	**most** *loyal*

The comparative and superlative forms of the common adjectives good and bad are formed in an irregular way.

Good	*better*	*best*
Bad	*worse*	*worst*

Building blocks at the end of nouns

The inflection suffix **S** is regularly added to the basic forms of nouns to indicate the **plural** form of the word, which indicates more than one example of the thing.

cats   *dogs*   *books*

> The plural form of some words is formed slightly differently, and the rules explaining how plurals are formed are given on pages 67–70.

Spelling words that contain suffixes

Adding a suffix that begins with a consonant, such as **LESS** or **SHIP**, to a root word is usually straightforward. Neither the root word nor the suffix is changed.

help + less = helpless

However, when adding a suffix that begins with a vowel, such as **ED** or **ABLE**, to a root word you need to take more care with the spelling. Depending on the ending of the root word, you may need to add an **E**, drop an **E**, double a consonant, or change a **Y** to an **I**.

cope + ed = coped
fit + ing = fitting
deny + able = deniable

> The rules for adding vowel suffixes are given in full on pages 63–64.

Double suffixes

Sometimes a suffix can have another suffix attached to it to make an even longer word.

> abuse + ive + ness = abusiveness
> accept + able + ness = acceptableness
> avail + able + ity = availability
> care + less + ly = carelessly
> commend + able + ly = commendably
> emotion + al + ism = emotionalism
> expense + ive + ly =expensively
> fear + less + ness = fearlessness

Greek and Latin roots

English has many words that contain Greek and Latin roots. Some of these roots appear in lots of different English words, and are still used regularly to create new words.

If you can get to know these roots, how to spell them and what they mean, you will find it a great help in your reading and writing, as well as in your spelling.

AER comes from Greek *aēr*, meaning 'air'. It is used in a lot of words connected with aircraft or aeronautics.

> **aero**plane   **aero**bics   **aero**dynamics

AMBI comes from the Latin word *ambo*, meaning 'both'.

> **ambi**dextrous   **ambi**valent

ANTHROP comes from the Greek word *anthrōpos*, meaning 'human being'.

    *anthrop*ology   phil*anthrop*ist   lyc*anthrop*y

AQUA is the Latin word for 'water'.

    *aqua*lung   *aqua*marine   *aqua*tic

Sometimes the second **A** in **AQUA** changes to another vowel.

    *aque*duct   *aque*ous   *aqui*fer

ASTRO comes from the Greek word *astron*, meaning 'star'.

    *astro*nomy   *astro*logy   *astro*naut

AUDI comes from the Latin word *audīre*, meaning 'to hear'.

    *audi*ence   *audi*tion   *audi*torium

BIO comes from the Greek word *bios*, meaning 'life'.

    *bio*logy   *bio*graphy   *bio*technology

CAPT and **CEPT** both come from the Latin word *capere*, meaning 'to take'.

    *capt*ure   *capt*ivate   *capt*ion
    con*cept*   inter*cept*   re*cept*ion

CEDE comes from the Latin word *cēdere*, meaning 'to go'.

    inter*cede*   pre*cede*   re*cede*

> Note that some words that sound like these do not have the same ending: pro*ceed*, suc*ceed*, super*sede*.

CENT comes from the Latin word *centum*, meaning 'hundred'. A *cent* is a monetary unit in many countries, taking its name from the fact that it is worth one hundredth of the main unit of currency.

*cent*ury   *cent*imetre   *cent*ipede

CLUDE comes from the Latin word *claudere*, meaning 'to close'.

con*clude*   ex*clude*   se*clude*d

CRED comes from the Latin word *crēdere*, meaning 'to believe'.

in*cred*ible   *cred*it   *cred*ulous

CYCL comes from the Latin word *cyclus*, which is itself derived from the Greek word *kuklos*, meaning 'circle' or 'wheel'.

re*cycl*able   *cycl*one   bi*cycle*

DEC comes from the Latin word *decem*, meaning 'ten'.

*dec*imal   *dec*ibel   *dec*ilitre

DICT comes from the Latin word *dīcere*, meaning 'to say'.

*dict*ionary   pre*dict*   contra*dict*

DOM comes from the Latin word *domus*, meaning 'house'.

*dom*estic   *dom*icile   *dom*e

DOMIN comes from the Latin word *dominus*, meaning 'master'.

*domin*ate   *domin*eering   con*domin*ium

DUCE and **DUCT** both come from the Latin word *ducere*, meaning 'to lead'.

intro**duce**	de**duce**	re**duce**
aque**duct**	con**duct**or	via**duct**

DUO is the Latin word for 'two'.

duo	**duo**poly	**duo**logue

EGO is the Latin word for 'I'.

ego	**ego**tist	**ego**centric

FACT comes from the Latin word *facere*, meaning 'to make'.

satis**fact**ion	**fact**ory	manu**fact**ure

FRACT comes from the Latin word *fractus*, meaning 'broken'.

fraction	**fract**ure	in**fract**ion

GEN comes from the Greek word *genesis*, meaning 'birth'.

gene	**gen**etics	**gen**esis

GEO comes from the Greek word *gē*, meaning 'earth'.

geology	**geo**metry	**geo**graphy

GRAPH comes from the Greek word *graphein*, meaning 'to write'.

graphic	auto**graph**	para**graph**

GRESS comes from the Latin word *gradī*, meaning 'to go'.

pro**gress**	di**gress**ion	ag**gress**ive

HYDRO comes from the Greek word *hudōr*, meaning 'water'. The word *hydro* also occurs on its own as a shortened form of *hydroelectric* and *hydrotherapy*.

      hydroplane   **hydro**foil   **hydro**therapy

Sometimes the **O** in **HYDRO** is dropped or changes to another vowel.

      hydrant   **hydra**ulic   de**hydra**ted

JECT comes from the Latin word *iacere*, meaning 'to throw'.

      in**ject**ion   de**ject**ed   re**ject**

KILO comes from the Greek word *chīlioi*, meaning 'a thousand'.

      kilometre   **kilo**gram   **kilo**watt

MANU comes from the Latin word *manus*, meaning 'hand'.

      manual   **manu**facture   a**manu**ensis

MILLI comes from the Latin word *mille*, meaning 'a thousand'.

      millimetre   **milli**gram   **milli**pede

MULTI comes from the Latin word *multus*, meaning 'many'.

      multiplication   **multi**cultural   **multi**storey

NOV comes from the Latin word *novus*, meaning 'new'.

      novelty   re**nov**ate   in**nov**ation

OCT comes from the Latin word *octō*, meaning 'eight'. The Greek word is *oktō*.

    ***oct**agon*   ***oct**ave*   ***oct**et*

PAED comes from the Greek word *pais*, meaning 'child'. The American spelling is **PED**. In British English it is pronounced to rhyme with *seed*. However, in America and Australia it rhymes with *said*.

    ***paed**iatrics*   ***paed**iatrician*   ***paed**ophile*

PED comes from the Latin word *pēs*, meaning 'foot'.

    ped**al*   ***ped**estal*   *quadru**ped

PED is also the American spelling of root **PAED**.

    ***ped**iatrics*   ***ped**iatrician*   ***ped**ophile*

PHIL comes from the Greek word *philos*, meaning 'loving'.

    phil**anthropist*   ***phil**osophy*   *Anglo**phile

PHOBIA comes from the Greek word *phobos*, meaning 'fear'. It appears in hundreds of words relating to the fear or hatred of certain people, animals, objects, situations and activities.

    *claustro**phobia***   *agora**phobia***   *xeno**phobia***

PHON comes from the Greek word *phōnē*, meaning 'sound' or 'voice'.

    phon**etic*   *sym**phon**y*   *micro**phone

PHOTO comes from the Greek word *phōs*, meaning 'light'.

    ***photo**copier*   ***photo**graph*   ***photo**sensitive*

POLY comes from the Greek word *polus*, meaning 'many' or 'much'. The word *poly* also occurs on its own as a shortened form of *polytechnic*, *polyester*, and *polythene*.

    polygon   **poly**styrene   **poly**gamy

PORT comes from the Latin word *portāre*, meaning 'to carry'.

    portable   im**port**   trans**port**ation

POS comes from the Latin word *positus*, meaning 'put'.

    position   im**pos**e   de**pos**it

PRIM comes from the Latin word *prīmus*, meaning 'first'.

    primary   **prim**itive   **prim**e

QUAD comes from the Latin word *quattuor*, meaning 'four'.

    quadrangle   **quad**ruped   **quad**riceps

SCOPE comes from the Greek word *skopein*, meaning 'to look at'.

    micro**scope**   tele**scope**   stetho**scope**

SCRIBE comes from the Latin word *scrībere*, meaning 'to write'. **SCRIPT** comes from the Latin word *scriptus*, meaning 'written', which is related to the word *scrībere*.

    scribe   sub**scribe**   de**scribe**
    script   sub**script**ion   de**script**ion

SECT comes from the Latin word *secāre*, meaning 'to cut'.

    section   dis**sect**   inter**sect**ion

SENT comes from the Latin word *sentīre*, meaning 'to feel'.

    sentimental   *consent*   *dissent*

SOC comes from the Latin word *socius*, meaning 'friend'.

    social   *association*   *sociology*

SON comes from the Latin word *sonāre*, meaning 'to sound'.

    sonic   *consonant*   *resonate*

STAT comes from the Latin word *stātus*, meaning 'standing', which itself comes from the verb *stāre*, meaning 'to stand'.

    statue   *static*   *status*

STRICT comes from the Latin word *stringere*, meaning 'to tighten'.

    strictness   *constrict*   *restriction*

STRUCT comes from the Latin word *struere*, meaning 'to build'.

    structure   *destructive*   *construction*

TACT comes from the Latin word *tangere*, meaning 'to touch'.

    tactile   *contact*   *intact*

TERR comes from the Latin word *terra*, meaning 'earth'.

    terrain   *Mediterranean*   *terrestrial*

THERM comes from the Greek word *thermē*, meaning 'heat'.

    thermometer   *thermal*   *hypothermia*

TRACT comes from the Latin word *tractus*, meaning 'dragged' or 'drawn'.

    *con***tract**   *sub***tract***ion*   **tract***or*

TRI comes from the Latin word *trēs*, meaning 'three'. The Greek word is *treis*.

    tri*angle*   **tri***o*   **tri***athlon*

VEN comes from the Latin word *venīre*, meaning 'to come'.

    ven*ue*   *con***ven***tion*   *inter***vene**

VERT comes from the Latin word *vertere*, meaning 'to turn'.

    *di***vert**   *re***vert**   *con***vert**

VIS comes from the Latin word *vīsus*, meaning 'sight', which itself comes from the verb *vidēre*, meaning 'to see'.

    vis*ual*   **vis***ible*   **vis***ion*
    vis*it*   *super***vise**   *tele***vis***ion*

VOR comes from the Latin word *vorāre*, meaning 'to devour'.

    vor*acious*   *carni***vore**   *omni***vor***ous*

Compound words

Many English words are formed quite simply by adding two existing words together. These are called **compound words**. It can be easy to spell these words if you break them down into their parts.

> *book + shop = bookshop*
> *door + mat = doormat*
> *summer + house = summerhouse*
> *tea + pot = teapot*
> *waist + coat = waistcoat*

Some words don't immediately seem as though they are made from two common words but in fact are. These can also be easy to spell if you think of them in terms of their two parts.

> *cup + board = cupboard*
> *hand + kerchief = handkerchief*
> *neck + lace = necklace*
> *pit + fall = pitfall*

Commonly occurring spelling patterns

Prefixes, suffixes and root forms all can be remembered as having a particular meaning. However, there are some combinations of letters that are useful to remember when learning English spelling but don't have any particular meaning.

The patterns in this section all come up in many different words and are not pronounced in the way you might expect. It is worth remembering these patterns and the common words in which they occur.

Some of these letter blocks were usually sounded in the original language (such as **OUGH** in Anglo-Saxon words or **IGN** in Latin words) but have lost their original sound in English as the pronunciation of the language has gradually become simplified.

The pattern **ALM** occurs in several words representing a sound that is more often spelt as **ARM**.

*al*mond	*balm*	*calm*
em*balm*	*palm*	qu*alm*
p*salm*		

The pattern **AUGHT** occurs in several words representing a sound that is more often spelt as **ORT**.

aught	*caught*	*daught*er
dis*traught*	*fraught*	*haught*y
naught	*naught*y	ons*laught*
s*laught*er	*taught*	

It also occurs in these words representing a sound that is more often spelt as **AFT**.

dr*aught*	*laught*er

The pattern **CH** occurs in many words that come from Greek representing a sound that is more often spelt as **C** or **K**.

a*ch*e	an*ch*or	bron*ch*itis
*ch*ameleon	*ch*aracter	*ch*arisma
*ch*asm	*ch*emical	*ch*emistry
*ch*iropodist	*ch*iropractor	*ch*lorine
*ch*olera	*ch*olesterol	*ch*ord
*ch*oreography	*ch*orus	*ch*risten
*Ch*ristmas	*ch*rome	*ch*ronic
monar*ch*	o*ch*re	psy*ch*iatry
psy*ch*ology	stoma*ch*	syn*ch*ronize

The pattern **CI** occurs before endings such as **OUS**, **ENT**, and **AL** in several words representing a sound that is more often spelt as **SH**. The root word often ends in **C** or **CE**.

artificial	atrocious	audacious
capricious	commercial	crucial
deficient	delicious	efficient
facial	fallacious	ferocious
financial	gracious	judicious
malicious	official	officious
pernicious	precious	precocious
proficient	racial	social
spacious	special	sufficient
suspicious	tenacious	vivacious

The pattern **EA** occurs in many words representing a sound that is more often spelt as **E**.

bread	breath	deaf
dead	dread	endeavour
head	heather	heaven
heavy	lead	meadow
ready	steady	sweat
thread	treacherous	tread
treasure	wealth	weather

The pattern **EAU** occurs in several words representing a sound that is more often spelt as **OW**. These words all come from French.

beau	bureau	chateau
gateau	tableau	

It also occurs in these words representing a sound that is more often spelt as **EW**.

beautiful	beauty

The pattern **EIGH** occurs in several words representing a sound that is more often spelt as **AY**.

eight	*freight*	*inveigh*
neigh	*neighbour*	*sleigh*
weigh	*weight*	

Less commonly, it can represent a sound that is more often spelt as **IE**.

height

The pattern **EIGN** occurs in several words representing a sound that is more often spelt as **AIN**.

deign	*feign*	*reign*

It also occurs in these words representing a sound that is more often spelt as **IN**.

foreign	*sovereign*

The pattern **GUE** occurs at the end of several words representing a sound that is more often spelt as **G**.

catalogue	*dialogue*	*epilogue*
fatigue	*harangue*	*intrigue*
league	*meringue*	*monologue*
plague	*rogue*	*synagogue*
tongue	*vague*	*vogue*

The pattern **IGH** occurs in several words representing a sound that is more often spelt as **IE**.

blight	*bright*	*fight*
flight	*fright*	*high*
light	*fight*	*might*

mi**gh**ty	ni**gh**t	pli**gh**t
ri**gh**t	si**gh**	si**gh**t
sli**gh**t	thi**gh**	ti**gh**t

The pattern **IGN** occurs in several words representing a sound that is more often spelt as **INE**.

al**ign**	ass**ign**	ben**ign**
cons**ign**	des**ign**	ens**ign**
mal**ign**	res**ign**	s**ign**

The pattern **OUGH** occurs in several words representing different pronunciations.

alth**ough**	bor**ough**	b**ough**
b**ough**t	br**ough**t	c**ough**
d**ough**	en**ough**	f**ough**t
n**ough**t	**ough**t	pl**ough**
r**ough**	s**ough**t	th**ough**
th**ough**t	thr**ough**	t**ough**
tr**ough**	wr**ough**t	

The pattern **OUL** occurs in several words representing a sound that is more often spelt as **OO**.

c**oul**d	sh**oul**d	w**oul**d

The pattern **OUR** occurs in several words representing a sound that is more often spelt as **ER**.

arm**our**	behavi**our**	clam**our**
col**our**	demean**our**	enam**our**ed
endeav**our**	fav**our**	ferv**our**
glam**our**	harb**our**	hon**our**
hum**our**	lab**our**	neighb**our**
parl**our**	ranc**our**	rig**our**
tum**our**	vap**our**	vig**our**

The pattern **OUS** occurs at the end of hundreds of words representing a sound that is more naturally spelt as **US**. Note that these words are invariably adjectives.

anx**ious**	caut**ious**	danger**ous**
fabul**ous**	fur**ious**	gener**ous**
hilari**ous**	joy**ous**	mountain**ous**
nerv**ous**	obv**ious**	pi**ous**
prev**ious**	ser**ious**	zeal**ous**

The pattern **QUE** occurs in several words representing a sound that is more often spelt as **C** or **K**.

anti**que**	che**que**	criti**que**
grotes**que**	masquerade	mos**que**
opa**que**	pictures**que**	pla**que**
statues**que**	techni**que**	uni**que**

The pattern **SC** occurs in many words representing a sound that is more often spelt as **S**.

ab**sc**ess	acquie**sce**	a**sc**ent
coale**sce**	cre**sc**ent	de**sc**ent
efferve**sc**ent	fa**sc**inate	ira**sc**ible
ob**sc**ene	o**sc**illate	re**sc**ind
scene	**sc**ent	**sc**ience
scimitar	**sc**intillate	**sc**issors

The pattern **SCI** occurs before a vowel in several words representing a sound that is more often spelt as **SH**.

con**sci**ence	con**sci**ous	lu**sci**ous

The pattern **TI** occurs before endings such as **OUS**, **ENT**, and **AL** in many words representing a sound that is more often spelt as **SH**.

ambitious	cautious	contentious
circumstantial	essential	facetious
infectious	nutritious	partial
patient	potential	quotient
residential	spatial	substantial

The pattern **TURE** occurs in many words representing a sound that is often spelt as **CHER**.

adventure	capture	creature
culture	denture	feature
fracture	furniture	future
gesture	lecture	mixture
moisture	nature	pasture
picture	puncture	texture
torture	venture	vulture

spelling rules

Spelling rules

English has a small number of rules that underpin how words and certain types of word ought to be spelt. If you can learn these rules, you will be on your way to becoming a better and more confident speller. Don't be put off if the rule sounds complicated – look at the examples and you will begin to see spelling patterns emerging.

Although these rules do not cover every word in the language, they can often help you make a good attempt at guessing how an unfamiliar word ought to be spelt.

Q is always followed by U

One of the simplest and most consistent rules is that the letter **Q** is always followed by **U**.

*qu*ick *qu*ack *qu*iet

> The only exceptions are a few unusual words that have been borrowed from other languages, especially Arabic: *burqa, Iraqi*.

J and V are followed by a vowel

These letters are rarely followed by a consonant and do not usually come at the ends of words.

If you come across a sound you think might be a **J** at the end of a word or syllable, it is likely to be spelt using the letters **GE** or **DGE**.

page *edge* *fora**ge***

If a word ends with the sound represented by **V**, there is likely to be a silent **E** after the **V**.

*recei**ve***   *gi**ve***   *lo**ve***

Double consonants don't occur at the start of a word

If a word begins with a consonant, you can be confident that it is a single letter.

> The only exceptions are a few unusual words that have been borrowed from other languages, such as *llama*.

H, J, K, Q, V, W, and X are not doubled

The consonants **B**, **C**, **D**, **F**, **G**, **L**, **M**, **N**, **P**, **R**, **S**, **T**, and **Z** are commonly doubled in the middle and at the end of words, but **H**, **J**, **K**, **Q**, **V**, **W**, **X** and **Y** are not, so you can be confident about them being single.

*re**j**oice*   *a**w**ake*   *le**v**el*

> There are occasional exceptions in compound words (such as *with**h**old* and *boo**kk**eeping*), words borrowed from other languages (such as *ti**kk**a*), and informal words (such as *sa**vv**y* and *bo**vv**er*).

A, I, and U don't come at the end of words

In general, English avoids ending words with **A**, **I**, and **U** and adds an extra letter to stop this happening.

say   *tie*   *due*

However, there are quite a lot of exceptions to this rule, most of which are words that have been borrowed from other languages.

banana   *ravioli*   *coypu*

The three-letter rule

'Content words' (words that name and describe things and actions) have at least three letters.

Words that do not name or describe things but exist to provide grammatical structure (prepositions, conjunctions and determiners) do not need to have as many letters as this.

This rule accounts for the fact that some content words have extra or doubled letters.

buy   *bee*   *inn*

Note that these extra letters are not found in non-content words with similar sounds.

by   *be*   *in*

> Two important exceptions to this rule are the verbs *do* and *go*.

I before E, except after C

When the letters **I** and **E** are combined to make the '**EE**' sound, the **I** comes before the **E**.

brief	chief	field
niece	siege	thief

When they follow the letter **C** in a word, the **E** comes before the **I**.

ceiling	deceit	receive

There are a few exceptions to this rule.

caffeine	protein	seize	weird

The rule does not hold true when the letters **I** and **E** combine to make a different sound from '**EE**'.

foreign	surfeit	their

Adding a silent E makes a short vowel become long

As noted on page 5, the vowels **A**, **E**, **I**, **O**, and **U** each have a 'short' sound when they appear on their own in short words.

cat	rat	hat
men	pen	ten
bit	hit	sit
dot	lot	got
but	nut	hut

Each of the vowels also has a characteristic 'long' sound, which is created by adding an **E** to the consonant after the vowel. The **E** is not sounded in these words.

date	rate	hate
scene	swede	theme
bite	mite	like
note	lone	mole
flute	rule	brute

If there is more than one consonant after a short vowel, adding a silent **E** does not make the vowel become long.

lapse	cassette	gaffe

C and G are soft before I and E but hard before A, O, and U

The letters **C** and **G** both have two sounds: one 'soft' and one 'hard'.

These letters always have a hard sound when they come before **A**, **O**, and **U**.

card	cot	recur
gang	gone	gum

Note that the word *margarine* is an exception to this rule.

In general these letters have a 'soft' sound before **I** and **E** (and also **Y**).

cent	circle	cycle
gentle	giraffe	gyrate

The rule is very strong for **C**, but there are a lot of exceptions for **G**.

gibbon	girl	get

Note that some words add a silent **U** after the **G** to keep the sound hard.

*gu*ess   *gu*ide   *gu*illotine
*gu*ilty   *gu*itar   fati*gue*

Adding endings to words ending in E

Many English words end with a silent **E**. When you add a suffix that begins with a vowel onto one of these words, you drop the **E**.

> abbreviat*e* + ion = abbreviation
> appreciat*e* + ive = appreciative
> desir*e* + able = desirable
> fortun*e* + ate = fortunate
> guid*e* + ance = guidance
> hop*e* + ing = hoping
> respons*e* + ible = responsible
> ventilat*e* + ed = ventilated

Words that end in **CE** and **GE** are an exception to this rule. They keep the final **E** before adding a suffix that begins with **A**, **O** or **U** in order to preserve the 'soft' sound.

> chang*e* + able = changeable
> notic*e* + able = noticeable
> advantag*e* + ous = advantageous

However you do drop the **E** in these words before adding a suffix that begins with **E**, **I** or **Y**.

> stag*e* + ed = staged
> notic*e* + ing = noticing
> chanc*e* + y = chancy

Adding the ending LY to words ending in LE

When you make an adverb by adding the suffix **LY** to an adjective that ends with **LE**, you drop the **LE** from the adjective.

> gent**le** + ly = gently
> id**le** + ly = idly
> subt**le** + ly = subtly

Adding endings to words ending in Y

When you add a suffix to a word that ends with a consonant followed by **Y**, you change the **Y** to **I**.

> appl**y** + ance = appliance
> beaut**y** + ful = beautiful
> craz**y** + ly = crazily
> happ**y** + ness = happiness
> smell**y** + er = smellier
> wooll**y** + est = woolliest

However, in certain short adjectives that end with a consonant followed by **Y**, you keep the **Y** when you add the ending **LY** to make an adverb.

> sh**y** + ly = shyly
> spr**y** + ly = spryly
> wr**y** + ly = wryly

Adding endings to words ending in C

You add a **K** to words that end in **C** before adding a suffix that begins with **I**, **E**, or **Y** in order to preserve the 'hard' sound.

> mimi**c** + ing = mimi**ck**ing
> froli**c** + ed = froli**ck**ed
> pani**c** + y = pani**ck**y

The word *arc* is an exception to this rule.

> *arc + ing = arcing*
> *arc + ed = arced*

When you make an adverb by adding the suffix **LY** to an adjective that ends with **IC**, you add **AL** after the **IC**.

> *basic + ly = basically*
> *genetic + ly = genetically*
> *chronic + ly = chronically*

The word *public* is an exception to this rule.

> *public + ly = publicly*

Adding endings to words ending in a single consonant

In **words of one syllable** ending in a short vowel plus a consonant, you double the final consonant when you add a suffix that begins with a vowel.

> *run + ing = running*
> *pot + ed = potted*
> *thin + est = thinnest*
> *swim + er = swimmer*

This does not apply to words ending in the consonants **H**, **J**, **K**, **Q**, **V**, **W**, **X** and **Y**, which are never doubled (see page 59).

> *slow + est = slowest*
> *box + er = boxer*

In **words of more than one syllable** ending in a single vowel plus a consonant, if the word is pronounced with the stress at the end, you double the final consonant when you add a suffix that begins with a vowel.

> *admit + ance = admittance*
> *begin + ing = beginning*
> *commit + ed = committed*
> *occur + ence = occurrence*

If the word does not have the stress at the end, the rule is that you don't double the final consonant when you add a suffix that begins with a vowel.

> *target + ed = targeted*
> *darken + ing = darkening*

However, when you add a suffix that begins with a vowel to a word that ends in a single vowel plus **L** or **P**, you always double the **L** or **P** regardless of the stress.

> *appal + ing = appalling*
> *cancel + ation = cancellation*
> *dial + er = dialler*
> *fulfil + ed = fulfilled*
> *handicap + ed = handicapped*
> *kidnap + er = kidnapper*
> *slip + age = slippage*
> *wrap + ing = wrapping*

The word *parallel* is an exception to this rule.

> *parallel + ed = paralleled*

Adding endings to words ending in OUR

There are a number of English words that end with the letters **OUR**.

colour   *glamour*   *humour*

When you add the suffix **ANT**, **ARY**, or **OUS** to these words, the **U** is dropped and **OUR** becomes **OR**.

colour + ant = colorant
glamour + ous = glamorous
humour + ous = humorous
honour + ary = honorary

When you add the suffix **ABLE** to these words, the **U** is not dropped.

honour + able = honourable
favour + able = favourable

Making plurals

The most common way to make a plural form of a word (to show that you are talking about more than one example of it) is simply to add an **S**.

dog + s = dogs
house + s = houses
bee + s = bees
banana + s = bananas

When you make a plural of a word that ends with **S**, **X**, **Z**, **SH** or **CH**, you add **ES**.

> bus + es = buses
> kiss + es = kisses
> lens + es = lenses
> fox + es = foxes
> jinx + es = jinxes
> buzz + es = buzzes
> rash + es = rashes
> match + es = matches
> ranch + es = ranches

When you make a plural of a word that ends with a consonant plus **Y**, you change the **Y** to **I** and add **ES**.

> fairy + es = fairies
> pantry + es = pantries
> quality + es = qualities
> spy + es = spies
> story + es = stories

However, when you make a plural of a word that ends with a **vowel** plus **Y**, you simply add **S**.

> boy + s = boys
> day + s = days
> donkey + s = donkeys
> guy + s = guys

When you make a plural of a word that ends with a single **O**, you usually just add an **S**.

> memo + s = memos
> solo + s = solos
> zero + s = zeros

However, there are a number of words that end with a single **O** that add **ES** when they are plural.

> *echo + es = echoes*
> *hero + es = heroes*
> *potato + es = potatoes*
> *tomato + es = tomatoes*
> *veto + es = vetoes*

Remember: My her**oes** eat potat**oes** and tomat**oes**.

When you make a plural of a word that ends in a single **F** (and some words that end in **FE**), you change the **F** (or **FE**) to **V** and add **ES**.

> *leaf + es = lea**ves***
> *elf + es = el**ves***
> *life + es = li**ves***

There are some exceptions to this rule.

> *belief + s = beliefs*
> *chef + s = chefs*
> *roof + s = roofs*

When you make a plural of a word that ends with **EAU**, you can add either **X** or **S**. Words that end with **EAU** are French words that have come into English. The **X** ending is the French plural, and the **S** ending is the English one. Both forms are acceptable for these words.

> *bureau + x = bureaux*
> *bureaus + s = bureaus*
> *chateau + x = chateaux*
> *chateau + s = chateaus*
> *gateau + x = gateaux*
> *gateau + s = gateaus*

Even when the **X** ending is used, these words are usually pronounced as though they end with an **S**, although the **X** can sometimes be treated as a silent letter (as it is in French).

The suffix FUL

The suffix that means 'full of' is spelt **FUL** – not (as you might expect) **FULL**. When you add the suffix onto an existing word to create a new word, the new word is always spelt with just one **L**.

beautiful	*cupful*	*faithful*
grateful	*hopeful*	*painful*

The prefix AL

When *all* and another word are joined to make an unhyphenated word, you drop the second **L**.

all + mighty = almighty
all + ready = already
all + though = although
all + together = altogether

However, if the word you make by adding *all* to another word is spelt with a hyphen, you keep both **L**'s.

all + important = all-important
all + inclusive = all-inclusive
all + powerful = all-powerful

The prefixes ANTE and ANTI

There are some English words that begin with **ANTE** and other words that begin with **ANTI**. You can usually work out how to spell the word if you think about what it means.

Words that begin with **ANTE** usually have a meaning of 'before' or 'in front of'.

> ***ante**cedent*   ***ante**diluvian*   ***ante**room*

Words that begin with **ANTI** usually have a meaning of 'against' or 'opposite'.

> ***anti**septic*   ***anti**social*   ***anti**matter*

The prefixes FOR and FORE

There are some English words that begin with **FOR** and other words that begin with **FORE**. You can often work out how to spell the word if you think about what it means.

Words that begin with **FORE** usually have a meaning of 'before' or 'in front of'.

> ***fore**cast*   ***fore**father*   ***fore**shore*

If the word does not have this meaning, it is likely that it will be spelt **FOR**, and there will not be an **E** after the **R**.

> ***for**give*   ***for**get*   ***for**feit*

The endings CE and SE

There are some English words that end in **CE** and have a related word that ends in **SE**. Sometimes the two words sound the same, and it can be easy to use the wrong spelling.

A useful general rule is that nouns are spelt with **CE** – think of the nouns *ice* and *advice* to help you remember.

> *a dog licence*
> *piano practice*

However, verbs that are related to these nouns end in **SE** – think of *advise* (where the pronunciation makes it obvious that the word is not spelt with **CE**).

> *licensed to kill*
> *to practise the drums*

The endings IZE and ISE

Historically, both **ISE** and **IZE** have been equally acceptable as suffixes forming verbs in English.

organize	*realize*	*pulverize*
organise	*realise*	*pulverise*

The same is true of related words.

organizer	*realization*	*pulverized*
organiser	*realisation*	*pulverised*

It is perfectly correct to use either a **Z** or an **S** in these words in British English, but you should be consistent and stick to one letter. However, the **IZE** spelling is preferred in American English. (Some people regard **IZE** as an Americanism, and object to its use in British English, but all leading British dictionary publishers show **IZE**, **IZATION**, and **IZER** as the main spelling form for these words.)

Some words are always spelt with **ISE**. These are usually words where the ending is a natural part of the word and has not been added on as a suffix.

advert*ise*	adv*ise*	chast*ise*
compr*ise*	comprom*ise*	desp*ise*
dev*ise*	disgu*ise*	exerc*ise*
improv*ise*	pr*ise*	rev*ise*
superv*ise*	surpr*ise*	telev*ise*

Some words are always spelt with **IZE**.

cap*size*	pr*ize*

Note the difference between *prise*, meaning 'to force open', and *prize*, meaning 'to value highly'.

Rules for using apostrophes

Showing possession

The apostrophe (') is used to show that something belongs to someone. It is usually added to the end of a word and followed by an **S**.

'S is added to the end of singular words.

> *a baby**'s** pushchair*
> *Hannah**'s** book*
> *a child**'s** cry*

'S is added to the end of plural words not ending in **S**.

> *children**'s** games*
> *women**'s** clothes*
> *people**'s** lives*

An apostrophe alone is added to plural words ending in **S**.

> *Your grandparents are your parents**'** parents.*
> *We are campaigning for workers**'** rights.*
> *They hired a new ladies**'** fashion guru.*

'S is added to the end of names and singular words ending in **S**.

> *James**'s** car*
> *the octopus**'s** tentacles*

Note, however, that if the word ending in **S** is a historical name, an apostrophe only is sometimes preferred.

> *Dickens**'** novels*
> *St Giles**'** Cathedral*

'S is added to the end of certain professions or occupations to indicate workplaces.

> *She is on her way to the doctor's.*
> *James is at the hairdresser's.*

'S is added to the end of people or their names to indicate that you are talking about their home.

> *I'm going over to Harry's for tea tonight.*
> *I popped round to Mum's this afternoon, but she wasn't in.*

To test whether an apostrophe is in the right place, think about who the owner is.

> *the boy's books [= the books belonging to the boy]*
> *the boys' books [= the books belonging to the boys]*

> Note that an apostrophe is *not* used to form possessive pronouns such as *its*, *yours*, or *theirs*. Nor is it used to form the plurals of words such as *potatoes* or *tomatoes*.

Showing a contraction

An apostrophe is used in shortened forms of words to show that one or more letters have been missed out. These contractions usually involve shortened forms of common verbs such as *be* and *have*.

> *I'm [short for 'I am']*
> *they've [short for 'they have']*
> *we're [short for 'we are']*

Some contractions involve the negative word *not*.

> *aren't [short for 'are not']*
> *isn't [short for 'is not']*
> *haven't [short for 'have not']*

> Note that the apostrophe is always positioned at the point where the omitted letters would have been.

An apostrophe is also used in front of two digits as a way of referring to a year or decade.

> *French students rioted in '68 [short for '1968'].*
> *He worked as a schoolteacher during the '60s and early '90s.*

Showing a plural

An apostrophe should *not* be used to form the plural of a normal word.

However, there is an exception to this rule. An apostrophe can be used in plurals of letters and numbers to make them easier to read.

> *Mind your p's and q's.*
> *His 2's look a bit like 7's.*
> *She got straight A's in her exams.*

Rules for using a capital letter

A capital (or 'upper-case') letter is used to mark the beginning of a sentence.

When I was 20, I dropped out of university and became a model.

Capital letters are also used for the first letter in proper nouns. These include:

- people's names
    Jenny Forbes   *William Davidson*

- days of the week
    Monday   *Wednesday*   *Saturday*

- months of the year
    August   *October*   *June*

- public holidays
    Christmas   *New Year*   *Yom Kippur*

- nationalities
    Spanish   *Iraqi*   *Argentine*

- languages
    Swahili   *Flemish*   *Gaelic*

- geographical locations
    Australia   *Loch Ness*   *Mount Everest*

- religions
    Islam   *Buddhism*   *Sikhism*

Capital letters are also used for the first letter in titles of books, magazines, newspapers, **TV** shows, films, etc. Where there are several words, a capital letter is usually used for each of the main 'content words' as well as the first word of the title.

The Times	*Hello!*	*Twelfth Night*
The Secret Garden	*Newsnight*	*Mamma Mia!*

tips for learning hard words

Tips for learning hard words

You can improve your spelling greatly by studying the rules and familiarizing yourself with the patterns that come up regularly. Nevertheless, knowing the principles of spelling can only get you so far. There are times when you just have to learn how the letters fall in a particular word.

The tips in this chapter can help you learn tricky spellings so that they stay in your mind.

Mnemonics

A **mnemonic** is a saying or rhyme that helps you remember something. The word comes from Greek *mnēmonikos*, which itself comes from *mnēmōn*, meaning 'mindful'. A mnemonic can be a rhyme or sentence that helps you remember anything, not just spelling. You may already know mnemonics for other things, for example **R**ichard **O**f **Y**ork **G**ives **B**attle **I**n **V**ain, which is often used as a way to remember the colours of the rainbow (because the first letters of each word correspond to the first letters of the colours red, orange, yellow, green, blue, indigo, and violet).

There are various types of mnemonics that can help with spelling.

Initial-letter mnemonics

In some mnemonics, the word you want to remember is spelt out by the initial letters of all the words in a sentence or phrase.

> **B**ig **e**lephants **a**re **u**seful **t**o **I**ndians **f**or **u**nloading **l**ogs.

This sentence can help you to remember the word *beautiful*.

Partial initial-letter mnemonics

In some mnemonics, a phrase just acts as a reminder of how to spell the tricky bits of a word, but does not spell out the whole word.

You can use this sort of mnemonic to remember how to spell the word *accelerate*.

> If it can **accele**rate, **a** **c**ar can **e**asily **l**ead **e**very race.

A similar device can be used to remember the double letters in the word *accommodation*.

> The **accomm**odation has **two** **c**ots and **two** **m**attresses.

Partial mnemonics

Another type of mnemonic uses words or syllables that are contained within the problem word to help you remember it.

You can use this technique to remember the beginning of the word *abattoir*.

> There may be **a** **batt**le in an **abatt**oir.

A similar device can be used to remember the double letters at the start of the word *address*.

> **Add** your **add**ress.

The remaining chapters of this book include many mnemonics to help you remember how to spell tricky words. Use these if you find they help you.

However, the best mnemonics are often ones that you make up yourself. If you base these phrases around words and topics that are especially meaningful to you, you are more likely to remember them. For example, you might use the names of your friends, your pets, or your family members, or you might make up sentences that relate to your hobbies. Try to make up your own mnemonics for words you find hard to remember.

Look, Say, Cover, Write, Check

Another way of learning how to spell a word is to go through five stages: look, say, cover, write, check.

- **Look** at the word carefully.

- **Say** the word aloud to yourself, listening to how it sounds.

- **Cover** the word and try to remember what it looks like.

- **Write** the word.

- **Check** what you have written to see if you got it right.

Breaking down the word into its parts

Another good way of learning a word is to break it down into its syllables, and sound them out, pronouncing even the silent letters.

> *dictionary = dic + ti + on + ar + y*
> *ecstasy = ec + sta + sy*
> *handkerchief = hand + ker + chief*
> *material = ma + te + ri + al*
> *separate = se + par + ate*
> *Wednesday = Wed + nes + day*

If you get into the habit of looking at words in this way you will find them easier to learn.

Word families

Words that come from the same root word tend to preserve the same core patterns in the spelling. If you know that one word is related to another word, it can help you remember how the word is spelt.

The words below are all related to *act*.

act	*action*	*activity*
re*act*	re*action*	re*active*

Sometimes knowing that words are related can help you remember which vowel to use. For example, words related to *irritate* all have an **A** after the **T**.

irritate	*irritant*	*irritable*

Word families are a very powerful way of remembering how to spell a word. However, there are just a few occasions when words that sound as though they might be related are in fact not related, or when words that are related are not spelt with the same core pattern. Some of these 'false friends' that you need to watch out for are listed on pages 149–152.

words
with
silent
letters

Words with silent letters

Some words are hard to spell because they contain letters that are not pronounced in speech. Often these letters were pronounced in the original language from which the word came into English. Here is a list of words that it is worth learning, including ways of remembering some of them.

abhor
> There is a silent **H** after the **B**.

> Remember: You ab**hor** something **hor**rible.

abscess
> There is a silent **C** after the first **S**.

acquaint, acquiesce, acquire, acquit
> There is a silent **C** before the **Q**.

aghast
> There is a silent **H** after the **G**.

> Remember: A**gh**ast at the **gh**osts.

almond
> There is a silent **L** before the **M**.

answer
> There is a silent **W** after the **S**.

asthma
> There is a silent **TH** after the **S**.

autumn
> There is a silent **N** after the **M**.

bankruptcy
>   There is a silent **T** after the **P**.

>   Remember that this word comes from *bankrupt* + the
>   ending *-cy*.

Buddhism
>   There is a silent **H** after the **DD**.

campaign
>   There is a silent **G** before the **N**.

castle
>   There is a silent **T** after the **S**.

column
>   There is a silent **N** after the **M**.

comb
>   There is a silent **B** after the **M**.

condemn
>   There is a silent **N** after the **M**.

>   Remember that this word is related to *condemnation*.

cupboard
>   There is a silent **P** before the **B**.

debt
>   There is a silent **B** before the **T**.

>   Remember that this word is related to *debit*.

descend
>   There is a silent **C** after the **S**.

>   Remember: You d**esc**end on an **esc**alator.

diaphragm
    There is a silent **G** before the **M**.
doubt
    There is a silent **B** before the **T**.

Remember that this word is related to *dubious*.

dumb
    There is a silent **B** after the **M**.
environment
    There is a silent **N** before the **M**.

Remember: There is **iron** in the envi**ron**ment.

exceed, excel, excellent, excess, excite
    There is a silent **C** after the **X**.
excerpt
    There is a silent **C** after the **X** and a silent **P** before the **T**.
exhaust, exhibit, exhilarate
    There is a silent **H** after the **X**.
extraordinary
    There is a silent **A** before the **O**.

Remember that this word comes from *extra + ordinary*.

fluorescent
    There is a silent **U** before the **O** and a silent **C** after the **S**.
foreign
    There is a silent **G** before the **N**.
ghastly, gherkin, ghetto, ghost, ghoul
    There is a silent **H** after the **G**.

gnarl, gnat, gnaw, gnome, gnu
> There is a silent **G** before the **N**.

government
> There is a silent **N** before the **M**.

handkerchief, handsome
> There is a silent **D** after the **N**.

honest, honour, hour
> There is a silent **H** at the start.

indict, indictment
> There is a silent **C** before the **T**.

> Remember: **I** **n**ever **d**abble **i**n **c**riminal **t**hings.

island, isle
> There is a silent **S** before the **L**.

jeopardize, jeopardy
> There is a silent **O** after the **E**.

knack, knee, kneel, knickers, knife, knight, knit, knob, knock, knot, know, knuckle
> There is a silent **K** before the **N**.

leopard
> There is a silent **O** after the **E**.

limb
> There is a silent **B** after the **M**.

listen
> There is a silent **T** after the **S**.

medieval
> There is a silent **I** after the **D**.

miniature
> There is a silent **A** before the **T**.

mnemonic
There is a silent **M** before the **N**.

> Remember: **M**y **n**ephew **E**ric **m**emorizes **o**dd **n**umbers **i**n **c**lass.

moreover
There is a silent **E** after the **O**.

mortgage
There is a silent **T** before the **G**.

muscle
There is a silent **C** after the **S**.

parliament
There is a silent **A** after the **I**.

playwright
There is a silent **W** before the **R**.

pneumatic, pneumonia
There is a silent **P** before the **N** at the beginning.

psalm
There is a silent **P** before the **S** and a silent **L** before the **M**.

pseudonym, psychedelic, psychiatry, psychic, psychology
There is a silent **P** before the **S**.

receipt
There is a silent **P** before the **T**.

rhetoric, rheumatism, rhinoceros, rhododendron, rhombus, rhubarb, rhyme, rhythm
There is a silent **H** after the **R** at the beginning.

sandwich
There is a silent **D** after the **N**.

scissors
There is a silent **C** after the first **S**.

sheikh
There is a silent **H** after the **K**.

shepherd
There is a silent **H** after the **P**.

> Remember that a shep**herd herd**s sheep.

silhouette
There is a silent **H** after the **L**.
solemn
There is a silent **M** before the **N**.
sovereign
There is a silent **G** before the **N**.
spaghetti
There is a silent **H** after the **G**.
stalk
There is a silent **L** before the **K**.
subtle
There is a silent **B** before the **T**.

> Remember: **Sub**marines move in **sub**tle ways.

sword
There is a silent **W** after the **S**.
talk
There is a silent **L** before the **K**.
two
There is a silent **W** after the **T**.
viscount
There is a silent **S** before the **C**.

> Remember: The **vi**s**count** gets a d**iscount**.

walk
There is a silent **L** before the **K**.
Wednesday
There is a silent **D** before the **N**.
what, when, where, whether, which, why
There is a silent **H** after the **W**.
wrangle, wrap, wrath, wreath, wreck, wrench, wrestle, wretched, wriggle, wring, wrinkle, write, wrist, wrong
There is a silent **W** before the **R**.
yoghurt
There is a silent **H** after the **G** in the usual spelling form.

single and double letters

Single and double letters

Some words present a problem in spelling because it is not obvious whether they have a double or single letter. Here is a list of words that it is worth learning, including ways of remembering some of them.

abattoir
> There is one **B** and two **T**'s.

> Remember: There may be a **batt**le in an a**batt**oir.

abbreviate
> There are two **B**'s.

accelerate
> There are two **C**'s and one **L**.

accessory
> There are two **C**'s and two **S**'s.

accident
> There are two **C**'s.

> Remember: **A c**lose **c**all can lead to an a**cc**ident.

accommodate
> There are two **C**'s and two **M**'s.

> Remember: If you think that this word **accommodates** as many letters as possible, it will help you to remember that there are the maximum number of **C**'s and **M**'s!

accompany
> There are two **C**'s.

accumulate
> There are two **C**'s and one **M**.

accurate
> There are two **C**'s and one **R**.

across
> There is one **C** and two **S**'s.

address
> There are two **D**'s and two **S**'s.

> Remember: **Add** your **add**ress.

affiliate
> There are two **F**'s and one **L**.

aggravate
> There are two **G**'s and one **V**.

aggressive
> There are two **G**'s and two **S**'s.

allergy
> There are two **L**'s.

> Remember: An **allergy** saps **all** energy.

alligator
> There are two **L**'s and one **G**.

already, although, altogether
> There is only one **L**.

aluminium
> There are no double letters.

appal
> There are two **P**'s and one **L**.

apparatus, apparent, appearance
> There are two **P**'s and one **R**.

appendix, appliance, appreciate, apprehensive, approve, approximate
> There are two **P**'s.

assassinate, assess
> There are two double **S**'s.

associate
> There are two **S**'s and one **C**.

attitude
> There is a double **T** followed by a single **T**.

> Remember: **At ti**mes you have a bad **atti**tude.

baggage
> There is a double **G** – just the same as in *luggage*.

balloon
> There are two **L**'s and two **O**'s.

> Remember: A **ball**oon is shaped like a **ball**.

banana
> There are two single **N**'s.

battalion
> There are two **T**'s and one **L** – just the same as in *battle*.

beginner
> There is one **G** and two **N**'s.

belligerent
> There are two **L**'s and one **G**.

boycott
> There are two **T**'s.

broccoli
> There are two **C**'s and one **L**.

> Remember: Bro**ccoli c**ures **coli**c.

bulletin
There are two **L**'s and one **T** – just the same as in *bullet*.

carafe
There is one **R** and one **F**.

career
There is no double **R**.

> Remember: A **car car**eered off the road.

cassette
There are two **S**'s and two **T**'s.

cinnamon
There are two **N**'s and one **M**.

collaborate
There are two **L**'s and one **B**.

colleague
There are two **L**'s.

colossal
There is one **L** in the middle and two **S**'s.

> Remember: Co**loss**al **loss**es

commemorate
There is a double **M** followed by a single **M**.

commercial
There are two **M**'s.

commiserate
There are two **M**'s and one **S**.

> Remember: You have to com**miser**ate with a **miser**.

commit
There are two **M**'s and one **T**.

committee
There are two **M**'s, two **T**'s, and two **E**'s.

> If you remember that a **committee** should have as many members as possible, it may help you remember that this word has the maximum number of **M**'s, **T**'s and **E**'s.

compel
There is only one **L**.

connotation
There are two **N**'s and two single **T**'s.

control
There is only one **L**.

coolly
There are two **L**'s.

correspond
There are two **R**'s.

curriculum
There are two **R**'s and one **C** in the middle.

daffodil
There are two **F**'s but no double **D**.

desiccated
There is one **S** and two **C**'s – which is the same as in **co**conut**s**!

deterrent
There are two **R**'s but no double **T**.

dilemma
There is one **L** and two **M**'s.

> Remember: **Emma** is in a dil**emma**.

disappear, disappoint, disapprove
There is one **S** and two **P**'s.

> Remember: Th**is app**le has d**isapp**eared.

dispel
There is one **S** and only one **L**.

dissatisfied
There are two **S**'s after the first **I**.

dissect
There are two **S**'s.

dissimilar
There are two **S**'s, one **M** and one **L**.

earring
There are two **R**'s.

effervescent
There are two **F**'s and one **S**.

eligible
There is only one **L** at the start.

> Remember: You must **el**ect the most **el**igible candidate.

embarrass
There are two **R**'s and two **S**'s.

> Remember: This word has two **R**'s and two **S**'s, which is an **embarrass**ment of riches!

enrol
There is only one **L**.

erroneous
There are two **R**'s and one **N**.

> Remember that this word is related to *err*.

exaggerate
There are two **G**'s.

> Remember: I am st**agger**ed that you ex**agger**ate.

excellent
There are two **L**'s.

> Remember: My **ex-cell**mate was an **excell**ent friend.

flammable
There are two **M**'s (unlike *flame*).

fulfil
There are two single **L**'s.

fullness
There are two **L**'s and two **S**'s.

giraffe
There is one **R** and two **F**'s.

guerrilla
There are two **R**'s and two **L**'s.

graffiti
There are two **F**'s and one **T**.

hallucination
There are two **L**'s, one **C**, and one **N**.

harass
There is one **R** and two **S**'s.

hazard
There is only one **Z** (unlike *blizzard*).

hideous
There is only one **D**.

> Remember: **Hide** that **hide**ous thing away.

holiday
There is only one **L** and one **D**.

> Remember that a hol**id**ay was originally a hol**y d**ay.

horrible
There are two **R**'s – just the same as in *terrible*.

horror
There is a double **R** – just the same as in *terror*.

hurricane
There are two **R**'s and one **C**.

illiterate
There are two **L**'s and a single **T**.

imitate
There are no double letters.

immediate
There are two **M**'s and one **D**.

inaccurate
There is one **N**, two **C**'s, and one **R**.

ineligible
There are no double letters.

innocent
There are two **N**'s and one **C**.

innocuous
There are two **N**'s and one **C**.

intelligence, intelligent
There are two **L**'s.

> Remember: I can **tell** the **gent** is in**tell**igent.

interrogate

There are two **R**'s and one **G**.

> Remember: In**terro**gation causes **terro**r.

interrupt

There are two **R**'s.

> Remember: It's **terri**bly rude to in**terr**upt.

irregular

There are two **R**'s and one **G**.

irrelevant

There are two **R**'s and one **L**.

irritable

There are two **R**'s and one **T**.

keenness

There are two **N**'s and two **S**'s.

limit

There is only one **M** and one **T**.

literature

There is only one **T**.

luggage

There is a double **G** – just the same as in *baggage*.

macabre

There is only one **C**.

macaroon

There is only one **C** and one **R**.

marvellous

There are two **L**'s.

mattress

There are two **T**'s and two **S**'s.

mayonnaise

There are two **N**'s.

> Remember: Dip **n**ice **n**ibbles in mayo**nn**aise.

medallist
> There is one **D** and two **L**'s.

> Remember that this word is made up of *medal + list.*

Mediterranean
> There is one **D**, one **T**, and two **R**'s.

millennium
> There are two **L**'s and two **N**'s.

millionaire
> There are two **L**'s and one **N**.

misshapen
> There are two **S**'s.

misspell
> There are two **S**'s and two **L**'s.

misspent
> There are two **S**'s.

necessary
> There is one **C** and two **S**'s.

> Remember: It is ne**cess**ary for a shirt to have **one c**ollar and **two s**leeves.

obsession, obsessive
> There is a single **S** followed by a double **S**.

occasion
> There are two **C**'s and one **S**.

occupy
> There are two **C**'s and one **P**.

occur
> There are two **C**'s and one **R**.

occurrence
> There are two **C**'s and two **R**'s.

omission
> There is one **M** and two **S**'s.

opinion
>There is one **P** and a single **N** in the middle.

opponent, opportunity, opposite
>There are two **P**'s.

overrate
>There are two **R**'s – just the same as in *underrate*.

paraffin
>There is one **R** and two **F**'s.

> Remember: Pa**r**a**ff**in **r**eally **f**uels **f**ires.

parallel
>There is a double **L** in the middle and a single **L** at the end.

pastime
>There is one **S** and one **T**.

penicillin
>There are two **L**'s and no double **N**.

> Remember: You take peni**cill**in when you are **ill**.

permit
>There is only one **T**.

personnel
>There are two **N**'s and one **L**.

porridge
>There are two **R**'s.

possess
>There are two double **S**'s.

> Remember: You should po**ss**e**ss** **two** **s**hoes and **two** **s**ocks.

possible
>There are two **S**'s.

preferred
> There is one **F** and a double **R**.

preference
> There is one **F** and no double **R**.

procedure
> There is only one **E** after the **C**.

profession, professor
> There is one **F** and two **S**'s.

profitable
> There is one **F** and one **T**.

propel
> There is a single **P** and a single **L**.

propeller
> There is a single **P** and a double **L**.

quarrel
> There are two **R**'s and one **L**.

questionnaire
> There are two **N**'s.

really
> There are two **L**'s.

rebellion
> There is one **B** and two **L**'s.

recommend
> There is one **C** and two **M**'s.

recurrent
> There is a single **C** and a double **R**.

referred
> There is a single **F** and a double **R**.

remittance
> There is one **M** and two **T**'s.

resurrection
> There is a single **S** and a double **R**.

sapphire
> There are two **P**'s.

Remember: You would be ha**pp**y to get a sa**pp**hire.

satellite
  There is one **T** and two **L**'s.

> Remember: **Tell** me about the sa**tell**ite.

settee
  There is a double **T** and a double **E**.

> Remember: **Sett**le down on the **sett**ee.

skilful
  There are two single **L**'s.

solicitor
  There are no double letters.

success
  There is a double **C** and a double **S**.

succinct
  There is a double **C**.

suddenness
  There is a double **D** and a double **N**.

sufficient
  There are two **F**'s.

suffocate
  There are two **F**'s and one **C**.

supplement
  There are two **P**'s and one **M**.

suppose
  There are two **P**'s.

suppress
  There is a double **P** and a double **S**.

surplus
  There is only one **S** at the end.

symmetry
  There are two **M**'s and one **T**.

taffeta
  There are two **F**'s and no double **T**.

tattoo
> There is a double **T** and a double **O**.

terrible
> There are two **R**'s – just the same as in *horrible*.

terror
> There is a double **R** – just the same as in *horror*.

threshold
> There is only one **H**.

toffee
> There are two **F**'s and two **E**'s.

tomorrow
> There is one **M** and two **R**'s.

tranquil
> There is only **L** at the end.

tranquillity
> There are two **L**'s.

tyranny
> There is one **R** and two **N**'s.

underrate
> There are two **R**'s – just the same as in *overrate*.

until
> There is only **L** at the end.

usually
> There are two **L**'s.

vacuum
> There is one **C** and two **U**'s.

vanilla
> There is one **N** and two **L**'s.

> Remember: **Vanill**a ice cream from the **van** made me **ill**.

verruca
> There are two **R**'s and one **C**.

villain
> There are two **L**'s.

walnut

There is only one **L** and one **T**.

welcome, welfare

There is only one **L**.

withhold

There are two **H**'s.

woollen

There are two **O**'s and two **L**'s.

words with foreign spelling patterns

Words with foreign spelling patterns

Some words present a problem in spelling because they have come into English from another language and have kept a spelling pattern found in the original language. Often these spelling patterns are quite different from the patterns you would expect to find in English words.

If you know a bit of French or Greek, for example, you will find it easier to understand why words that come from those languages are spelt the way they are. Even if you don't, you should soon get used to certain spelling patterns from these languages that come up repeatedly in English, such as **EAU** and **EUR** in French words and **AE** and **RRH** in Greek words.

Here is a list of words that it is worth learning, including ways of remembering some of them.

abattoir
 The ending is **OIR**. The word comes from French.
amateur
 The ending is **EUR**. The word comes from French.
apparatus
 The ending is **US** (not **OUS**). The word comes from Latin.
archaeology
 The second syllable is spelt **CHAE**. The word comes from Greek.

> Remember: Ar**chae**ology discovers **c**urious **h**ouses of **a**ncient **e**ras.

beautiful, beauty
 The beginning is **BEAU**. These words come from French.

> Remember: **B**ig **e**ars **a**re **u**seful.

biscuit
The ending is **CUIT**. The word comes from French (where *cuit* means 'cooked').

> Remember: If you want a bisc**uit**, I will give **u it**.

bouquet
The first vowel sound is spelt **OU**, the middle consonant is **Q**, and the ending is **ET**. The word comes from French.

> Remember: A bou**qu**et for the **que**en.

bourgeois
The first vowel sound is spelt **OUR**, the consonant in the middle is **GE**, and the ending is **OIS**. The word comes from French.

braille
The ending is **AILLE**. The word comes from a French name.

brochure
The ending is **CHURE**. The word comes from French.

brusque
The ending is **SQUE**. The word comes from French.

bureau
The ending is **EAU**. The word comes from French.

> Remember: **B**usinesses **u**sing **r**otten **e**thics **a**re **u**seless.

camouflage
The vowel sound in the middle is spelt **OU**, and the ending is **AGE**. The word comes from French.

catarrh
The ending is **ARRH**. The word comes from Greek.

champagne
The opening is **CH** and the ending is **AGNE**. The word comes from a French place-name.

chaos

The opening sound is spelt **CH**. The word comes from Greek.

> Remember: **C**riminals **h**ave **a**bandoned **o**ur **s**ociety.

character

The opening sound is spelt **CH**. The word comes from Greek.

chauffeur

The opening is **CH** and the ending is **EUR**. The word comes from French.

chord, chorus

The opening sound is spelt **CH**. These words come from Greek.

chute

The opening is **CH**. The word comes from French.

connoisseur

The middle vowel sound is spelt **OI** and the final vowel sound is spelt **EUR**. The word comes from French. (Also watch out for the double **N** and double **S**!)

crèche

The ending is **CHE**, and the word is usually spelt with an accent over the first **E**. The word comes from French.

crochet

The ending is **CHET**. The word comes from French.

curriculum vitae

The ending is **AE**. The term comes from Latin.

dachshund

The middle is **CHSH**. The word comes from German (where *Dachs* means 'badger' and *Hund* means 'dog').

> Remember: Da**chshund**s **ch**ase **sh**eep through the **und**ergrowth.

diarrhoea

The middle is **RRHOE**. The word comes from Greek.

etiquette
> The ending is **QUETTE**. The word comes from French.

euphoria, euthanasia
> The opening is **EU**. These words come from Greek (where *eu* means 'well').

Fahrenheit
> There is an **H** before the **R**, and the ending is **EIT**. The word comes from a German name.

fiancé, fiancée
> The ending is **CÉ** when referring to a man and **CÉE** when referring to a woman. The word comes from French.

foyer
> The ending is **ER**. The word comes from French.

gateau
> The ending is **EAU**. The word comes from French.

grandeur
> The ending is **EUR**. The word comes from French.

haemorrhage
> The first vowel sound is spelt **AE**, and the middle is **ORRH**. The word comes from Greek.

hierarchy, hieroglyphics
> The beginning is **HIER**. These words come from Greek (where *hieros* means 'holy').

> Remember: **H**idden **i**n **E**gyptian **r**uins.

hypochondriac, hypocrisy, hypocrite
> The beginning is **HYPO**. These words come from Greek (where *hypo* means 'under').

jodhpur
> There is a silent **H** after the **D** and the ending is **UR**. The word comes from a place-name in India.

> Remember: You wear jo**dh**purs when you ride a **d**appled **h**orse.

karate

The final letter is **E**. The word comes from Japanese.

khaki

There are two **K**'s and a silent **H**. The word comes from Urdu.

larynx

The ending is **YNX**. The word comes from Greek.

lasagne

The ending is **AGNE**. The word comes from Italian.

lieutenant

The first vowel sound is spelt **IEU**. The word comes from French (where *lieu* means 'place').

liqueur

The ending is **QUEUR**. The word comes from French.

manoeuvre

The vowel sound in the middle is spelt **OEU**. The word comes from French. The American spelling is *maneuver*.

martyr

The ending is **YR**. The word comes from Greek.

matinée

The ending is **ÉE** – just the same as in *fiancée*. The word comes from French.

meringue

The ending is **INGUE**. The word comes from French.

moustache

The first vowel sound is spelt **OU** and the ending is **CHE**. The word comes from French. The American spelling is *mustache*.

> Remember: A **mou**sta**che** is between the **mou**th and **che**ek.

naïve

The middle of this word is **AÏ**. The word comes from French.

niche

The ending is **ICHE**. The word comes from French.

nuance

The vowel after **U** is **A**. The word comes from French.

omelette

There is an **E** after the **M** and the ending is **ETTE**. The word comes from French.

pseudonym

There is a silent **P** at the beginning, the first vowel sound is spelt **EU**, and the ending is **NYM**. The word comes from Greek.

psychiatry, psychic, psychology

There is a silent **P** at the beginning, the first vowel is a **Y**, and there is an **H** after the **C**. These words come from Greek (where *psyche* means 'soul').

queue

The sequence of vowels is **UEUE**. The word comes from French, where it means 'tail'.

reconnaissance

The third vowel sound is spelt **AI**. The word comes from French. (Also watch out for the double **N** and double **S** – just the same as in *connoisseur*.)

rendezvous

The first vowel sound is spelt **E**, the second is spelt **EZ**, and the ending is **OUS**. The word comes from French.

repertoire

The middle vowel sound is spelt **ER** and the ending is **OIRE**. The word comes from French.

reservoir

The middle vowel sound is spelt **ER** and the ending is **OIR**. The word comes from French.

restaurant

The middle vowel sound is spelt **AU** and the ending is **ANT**. The word comes from French.

restaurateur

There is no **N** before the second **T** (unlike in *restaurant*), and the ending is **EUR**. The word comes from French.

rheumatism

The opening is **RHEU**. The word comes from Greek.

rhinoceros

The opening is **RH**, and the ending is **OS**. The word comes from Greek.

schizophrenia

The opening is **SCH**, and the next consonant sound is spelt **Z**.
The word comes from Greek (where *schizein* means 'to split').

sheikh

The vowel sound is spelt **EI**, and there is a silent **H** at the end.
The word comes from Arabic.

silhouette

There is a silent **H** after the **L**, the middle vowel is spelt **OU**, and the
ending is **ETTE**. The word comes from French.

souvenir

The first vowel sound is spelt **OU** and the ending is **IR**. The word
comes from French.

spaghetti

There is a silent **H** after the **G** and the ending is **ETTI**. The word
comes from Italian (as does *confetti*, which has a similar ending).

suede

The ending is **UEDE**. The word comes from French (where *de Suède*
means 'Swedish').

> Remember: **Sue de**manded **suede** shoes.

surveillance

The middle vowel sound is spelt is **EI**. The word comes from French.

yacht

The middle is **ACH**. The word comes from Dutch.

confusable words

Confusable words

When two words have a similar or identical sound, it is easy to confuse them and use the correct spelling for the wrong word. This section lists sets of words that are easily confused and offers some ways of remembering which is which.

accept, except

To **accept** something is to receive it or agree to it. **Except** means 'other than' or 'apart from'.

> Please **accept** my apologies
> The king would not **accept** their demands.
> I never wear a skirt **except** when we go out.

affect, effect

To **affect** something is to influence or change it. An **effect** is a result something gives or an impression something makes.

> Tiredness **affected** his concentration.
> discoveries which have a profound **effect** on medicine

Remember: To **a**ffect something is **a**lter it but the **e**ffect is the **e**nd result.

aid, aide

Aid means 'help', and to **aid** somebody is to help them. An **aide** is person who acts as an assistant to an important person.

> bringing **aid** to victims of drought
> They used bogus uniforms to **aid** them in the robbery.
> one of the President's **aides**

allude, elude

To **allude** to something is to refer to it in an indirect way. If something **eludes** you, you can't understand or remember it, and if you **elude** something, you dodge or escape from it.

*I never **allude** to that unpleasant matter.*
*The name of the tune **eludes** me.*
*She managed to **elude** the police.*

> Remember: If something **e**ludes you it **e**scapes you.

altar, alter

An **altar** is a holy table in a church or temple. To **alter** something is to change it.

*The church has a magnificent **altar**.*
*We may have to **alter** our plans.*

ascent, assent

An **ascent** is an upwards climb. To **assent** to something is to agree to it, and **assent** means 'agreement'.

*the **ascent** of Mount Everest*
*We all **assented** to the plan.*
*You have my whole-hearted **assent**.*

aural, oral

Something that is **aural** is to do with the ear or listening. Something that is **oral** is to do with the mouth or speaking.

*a good **aural** memory*
***oral** history*

> Remember: An **au**ral examination might involve **au**dio equipment.

base, bass

The **base** of something is the bottom part of it. A **bass** voice or instrument is the one that produces the lowest musical notes.

> the **base** of the table
> a **bass** guitar

baited, bated

If something such as a hook is **baited** it has food attached to it as a temptation. The word **bated** means 'cut short', and is mainly used in the expression *bated breath*.

> The trap had been **baited**.
> I waited with **bated** breath.

berth, birth

A **berth** is a bed on a ship or train, or a place where a ship is tied up. The **birth** of someone or something is the act of it being born or created.

> a cabin with six **berths**
> the date of her **birth**
> the **birth** of jazz

born, borne

To be **born** is to be brought into life. To be **borne** is to be accepted or carried, and when fruit or flowers are **borne** by a plant, they are produced by it. If something is **borne** out, it is confirmed.

> Olivia was **born** in Leicester.
> He has **borne** his illness with courage.
> The trees have **borne** fruit.
> The predictions have been **borne** out by the election results.

bough, bow

To **bow** is to bend your body or head, and a **bow** is an action where you bend your body or head. A **bough** is a branch of a tree.

*He gave a long **bow** to the king.*
*overhanging **boughs** of elm and ash*

boulder, bolder

A **boulder** is large rock. The word **bolder** means 'more brave' or 'more daring'.

*The road was blocked by an enormous **boulder**.*
*The victory made the soldiers feel **bolder**.*

brake, break

A **brake** is a device for slowing down, and to **brake** is to slow down by using this device. To **break** something is to change it so that it does not work or exist.

*I slammed on the **brakes**.*
***Brake** when you approach the junction.*
*to **break** a vase*

breach, breech

To **breach** something is to break or break through it, and a **breach** is a break or a gap made. The **breech** is the lower part of a human body, a rifle, or some other thing.

*a **breach** of the peace*
*a **breech** birth*

breath, breathe

Breath, without an **E**, is the noun, but **breathe**, with an **E**, is the verb.

*He took a deep **breath**.*
*I heard him **breathe** a sigh of relief.*

bridal, bridle

Bridal means 'relating to a bride'. A **bridle** is a piece of equipment for controlling a horse, and to **bridle** at something means to show anger about it.

> *a **bridal** dress*
> *a leather **bridle***
> *I **bridled** at the suggestion that I had been dishonest.*

broach, brooch

To **broach** a difficult subject means to introduce it into a discussion. A **brooch** is an item of jewellery.

> *Every time I **broach** the subject, he falls silent.*
> *a diamond **brooch***

callous, callus

Someone who is **callous** does not take other people's feelings into account. A **callus** is a patch of hard skin.

> *He treats her with **callous** indifference.*
> *Wearing high heels can cause **calluses**.*

canvas, canvass

Canvas is strong cloth. To **canvass** is to persuade people to vote a particular way or to find out their opinions about something.

> *a **canvas** bag*
> *The store decided to **canvass** its customers.*

Remember: If you canva**ss** you **s**eek **s**omething.

caught, court
Caught means 'captured'. A **court** is an enclosed space, such as one used in legal cases or to play tennis.

> *They never **caught** the man who did it.*
> *Silence in **court**!*

cereal, serial
Cereal is food made from grain. A **serial** is something published or broadcast in a number of parts. **Serial** also describes other things that happen in a series.

> *my favourite breakfast **cereal***
> *a new drama **serial***
> *a **serial** offender*

> Remember: A ser**i**al is part of ser**i**es, but a ce**real** is a **real** breakfast.

cheetah, cheater
A **cheetah** is a kind of wild cat. A **cheater** is someone who cheats.

> *a pack of **cheetahs** at the safari park*
> *He was exposed as a **cheater**.*

chord, cord
A **chord** is a group of three or more musical notes played together. **Cord** is strong thick string or electrical wire. Your vocal **cords** are folds in your throat which are used to produce sound.

> *playing major and minor **chords***
> *tied with a thick **cord***

> Remember: A **chor**d is part of a **chor**us.

chute, shoot

A **chute** is a steep slope for sliding things down. To **shoot** something means to send a missile at it, and to **shoot** means to go very fast.

> a rubbish **chute**
> **shooting** at pigeons
> to **shoot** along the ground

coarse, course

Coarse means 'rough' or 'rude'. A **course** is something that you go round, or a series of things you do on a regular basis. **Course** is also used in the phrase *of course*.

> a **coarse** fabric
> his **coarse** jokes
> a golf **course**
> a **course** of lectures
> Of **course** I want to go with you.

colander, calendar

A **colander** is a bowl-shaped drainer. A **calendar** is a chart with dates on it.

> Strain the potatoes with a **colander**.
> a **calendar** with Scottish scenes

> Remember: A col**and**er has h**and**les and drains wat**er**, while the cal**end**ar marks the **end** of the ye**ar**.

complement, compliment

A **complement** is something which goes well with something else or completes it, and to **complement** something is to go well with it or complete it. A **compliment** is a remark expressing admiration, and to **compliment** something is to express admiration for it.

> She is a perfect **complement** to her husband.
> It's always good to pass the odd **compliment**.

> Remember: A compl**i**ment is the opposite of an **i**nsult and a compl**e**ment compl**e**tes something.

confidant, confident

A **confidant** is a friend you tell secrets to. **Confident** means 'trusting' or 'self-assured'.

> *a trusted **confidant***
> *We are **confident** you will do a good job.*

council, counsel

A **council** is a group of people elected to look after the affairs of an area. **Counsel** is advice and to **counsel** is to give advice.

> *the parish **council***
> *I **counselled** her to forgive him.*

> Remember: The coun**cil** members take minutes with pen**cils**.

currant, current

A **currant** is a small dried grape. A **current** is a flow of water, air, or electricity. **Current** also means happening.

> *a **currant** bun*
> *an electrical **current***

> Remember: There are curr**a**nts in c**a**kes and curr**e**nts in **e**lectricity.

dairy, diary

A **dairy** is a shop selling milk, cream, and cheese. **Dairy** products are foods made from milk. A **diary** is a small book in which you keep a record of appointments.

> *She worked in a **dairy**.*
> *Make a note in your **diary**.*

Remember: The d**air**y next to the **air**port.

decease, disease

The word **decease** means 'to die'. A **disease** is an unhealthy condition.

> *my **deceased** father*
> *an infectious **disease***

Remember that if you are de**ceased** you have **ceased** to be.

defuse, diffuse

To **defuse** something is to make it less dangerous or tense. To **diffuse** something is to spread it or cause it to scatter. **Diffuse** means spread over a wide area.

> *Police **defused** a powerful bomb.*
> *The King will try to **defuse** the crisis.*
> *The message was **diffused** widely.*
> *curtains to **diffuse** the glare of the sun*

dependant, dependent

Dependant is the noun. **Dependent** is the adjective.

> *The child is her **dependant**.*
> *a **dependent** child*

desert, dessert

A **desert** is a region of land with little plant life. To **desert** someone is to abandon them. A **dessert** is sweet food served after the main course of a meal.

> the Sahara **Desert**
> She **deserted** me to go shopping.
> We had apple pie for **dessert**.

> Remember: A de**ss**ert is a **s**ticky **s**weet.

device, devise

Device, with a **C**, is the noun. **Devise**, with an **S**, is the verb.

> a safety **device**
> The schedule that you **devise** must be flexible.

disc, disk

A **disc** is a flat round object. A **disc** can be a storage device used in computers, and also a piece of cartilage in your spine. **Disk** is the usual American spelling for all senses of this word, except in the name **compact disc**, which is always spelt with a **C**. The spelling **disk** is sometimes preferred in British English when referring to the computer storage device.

discreet, discrete

If you are **discreet** you do not cause embarrassment with private matters. **Discrete** things are separate or distinct.

> We made **discreet** enquiries.
> The job was broken down into several **discrete** tasks.

> Remember: When discr**ete** means 'separate', the **E**'s are separate.

draft, draught

A **draft** is an early rough version of a speech or document. A **draught** is a current of cold air or an amount of liquid you swallow. **Draughts** is a popular board-game. A person who draws plans is a **draughtsman**.

> *a **draft** of the president's speech*
> *There is an unpleasant **draught** in here.*
> *a game of **draughts***
> *He worked as a **draughtsman**.*

> Remember: A dr**aft** is **a** **f**irst **t**ry, and a dra**ugh**t goes thro**ugh** a room.

elegy, eulogy

An **elegy** is a mournful song or poem. A **eulogy** is a speech praising someone or something.

> ***elegies** of love and loss*
> *a nostalgic **eulogy** to Victorian England*

elicit, illicit

To **elicit** something such as information means to draw it out. If something is **illicit** it is not allowed.

> *I managed to **elicit** the man's name.*
> ***illicit** drugs*

eligible, illegible

Eligible means 'suitable to be chosen for something'. If something is difficult to read it is **illegible**.

> *an **eligible** candidate*
> ***illegible** handwriting*

> Remember: **El**igible means suitable to be chosen, and so is related to the word **el**ect.

emigrate, immigrate
If you **emigrate** you leave a country to live somewhere else. Someone who does this is an **emigrant**. If you **immigrate** you enter a country to live there. Someone who does this is an **immigrant**.

> *Her parents had **emigrated** from Scotland.*
> *Russian **immigrants** living in the United States*

> Remember: **I**mmigrants come **in**.

eminent, imminent
Someone who is **eminent** is well-known and respected. **Imminent** means 'about to happen'.

> *an **eminent** professor*
> *an **imminent** disaster*

emit, omit
If something is **emitted** it is let out. If you **omit** something you leave it out. Similarly, something that is let out or sent out is an **emission**, while something that is left out is an **omission**.

> *cars **emitting** exhaust fumes*
> *She was **omitted** from the team.*
> *a programme to cut carbon **emissions***
> *a surprising **omission** from the list of great painters...*

enquire, inquire
These are alternative spellings for the same word. You can spell this word with an **E** or an **I**, although the form **inquire** is more common. Some people use the form **enquire** to mean 'ask about' and the form **inquire** to mean 'investigate'.

ensure, insure

To **ensure** something happens is to make sure that it happens. To **insure** something is to take out financial cover against its loss. To **insure** against something is to do something in order to prevent it or protect yourself from it.

> *His performance **ensured** victory for his team.*
> *You can **insure** your cat or dog for a few pounds.*
> *Football clubs cannot **insure** against the cancellation of a match.*

envelop, envelope

Envelop is the verb meaning 'to cover or surround'. **Envelope**, with an E at the end, is the noun meaning 'a paper covering which holds a letter'.

> *Mist began to **envelop** the hills.*
> *a self-addressed **envelope***

exercise, exorcize

To **exercise** means to move energetically, and **exercise** is a period of energetic movement. To **exorcize** an evil spirit means to get rid of it.

> Remember: You ex**e**rcise your l**e**gs but ex**o**rcize a gh**o**st.

faun, fawn

A **faun** is a legendary creature. A **fawn** is a baby deer. **Fawn** is also a pale brown colour, and to **fawn** on or over someone is to flatter them.

> *a story about **fauns** and centaurs*
> *Bambi the **fawn***
> *a **fawn** jumper*
> ***fawning** over his new boss*

final, finale

Final means 'last of a series', and a **final** is the last game or contest in a series to decide the winner. A **finale**, with an E at the end, is the finish of something, especially the last part of a piece of music or a show.

*the World Cup **Final***
*a fitting **finale** to the process*
*the **finale** of a James Bond film*

flare, flair
Flair is ability. A **flare** is a bright firework, and to **flare** is also to widen out.

*She showed natural **flair**.*
***flared** trousers*

flour, flower
Flour is used in baking. A **flower** is the coloured part of a plant.

*self-raising **flour***
*a basket of **flowers***

> Remember: Fl**ou**r makes bisc**u**its and d**u**mplings.

forgo, forego
To **forgo** means to choose not to have something. To **forego** is a less common word meaning 'to go before'.

*I decided to **forgo** the pudding.*
*I will ignore the **foregoing** remarks.*

fowl, foul
Foul means dirty or unpleasant, and a **foul** is also an illegal challenge in a sport. **Fowl** are certain types of birds which can be eaten.

***foul** play*
*booked for a bad **foul***
*a shop selling wild **fowl***

> Remember: An **owl** is a f**owl** but fo**u**l is **u**npleasant.

gambol, gamble
To **gambol** means to run about friskily. To **gamble** means to accept a risk, and a **gamble** is a risk that you take.

> lambs **gambolling** on the hillside
> to **gamble** on horses
> Going there would be an enormous **gamble**.

gorilla, guerrilla
A **gorilla** is a large ape. A **guerrilla** is a member of a small unofficial army fighting an official one.

> a documentary about **gorillas** and chimps
> ambushed by a band of **guerrillas**

> Remember: King K**o**ng was a giant g**o**rilla.

grate, great
A **grate** is a framework of metal bars, and to **grate** means to shred. **Great** means 'very large' or 'very good'.

> the **grate** over the drain
> **grated** cheese
> a **great** expanse of water
> the **great** composers

grill, grille
A **grill** is a device for cooking food, and to **grill** food is to cook it in such a device. A **grille** is a metal frame placed over an opening.

> Cook the meat under the **grill**.
> **Grill** it for ten minutes.
> iron **grilles** over the windows

grisly, grizzly
Grisly means nasty and horrible. **Grizzly** means grey or streaked with grey. A **grizzly** is also a type of bear.

> *grisly murders*
> *a grizzly beard*

hangar, hanger
A **hangar** is a place where aeroplanes are kept. A **hanger** is a device for storing clothes in a wardrobe.

> *a row of disused aircraft hangars*
> *Put your coat on a hanger.*

hear, here
To **hear** is to become aware of a sound with your ears. Something that is **here** is in, at or to this place or point.

> *Can you hear me?*
> *We come here every Summer.*

heir, air
An **heir** is someone who will inherit something. **Air** is the collection of gases that we breathe.

> *His heir received a million pounds.*
> *polluted air*

heroin, heroine
Heroin is a powerful drug. The **heroine** of a story is the main female character in it.

> *addicted to heroin*
> *the heroine of the film*

hoard, horde
To **hoard** is to save things, and a **hoard** is a store of things that have been saved. A **horde** is a large group of people, animals, or insects.

>   a priceless **hoard** of modern paintings
>   a **horde** of press photographers

hour, our
An **hour** is a period of time. **Our** means 'belonging to us'.

>   a journey of four **hours**
>   **our** favourite coffee shop

humus, hummus
Humus is decaying vegetable material in the soil. **Hummus** is a food made from chickpeas.

>   soil enriched with **humus**
>   a lunch of salad and **hummus**

Hungary, hungry
Hungary is a European country. It is spelt with an **A**, unlike **hungry**, which means 'wanting to eat'.

> Remember: **Gary** from Hun**gary** gets an**gry** when he is hun**gry**.

idol, idle
An **idol** is a famous person worshipped by fans, or a picture or statue worshipped as a god. **Idle** means 'doing nothing'.

>   the **idol** of the United supporters
>   The villagers worshipped golden **idols**.
>   He's an **idle** layabout.

> Remember: To be id**le** takes **l**ittle **e**nergy.

it's, its
It's, with an apostrophe, is a shortened form of *it is*. **Its**, without an apostrophe, is used when you are referring to something belonging or relating to things that have already been mentioned.

> *It's cold.*
> *The lion lifted its head.*

jewel, dual
A **jewel** is a precious stone. **Dual** means 'consisting of two parts'.

> *a box full of jewels*
> *a dual carriageway*

kerb, curb
A **kerb** is the raised area at the side of road. To **curb** something means to restrain it.

> *The car mounted the kerb.*
> *I tried to curb my enthusiasm.*

In American English, **curb** is the spelling for both meanings.

kernel, colonel
A **kernel** is a seed or part of a nut. A **colonel** is an army officer.

> *apricot kernels*
> *a colonel in the French army*

Remember: The co**lonel** is a **lonel**y man.

know, now
To **know** something means to be certain that it is true. **Now** means 'at this moment'.

> *Do you know the way to the bus station?*
> *I'm just leaving now.*

leant, lent
Leant is the past tense of the verb **lean**. **Lent** is the past tense of the verb **lend**.

> She **leant** back in her chair.
> She was **lent** Maureen's spare wellingtons.

led, lead
Led is the past tense of the verb **lead**. **Lead**, when it is pronounced like **led**, is a soft metal, or the part of a pencil that makes a mark.

> the road which **led** to the house
> **lead** poisoning

licence, license
Licence, ending in **CE**, is the noun. **License**, ending in **SE**, is the verb.

> a driver's **licence**
> a TV **licence**
> Censors agreed to **license** the film.
> They were **licensed** to operate for three years.

lightening, lightning
Lightening is a form of the verb **lighten**, and means 'becoming lighter'.
Lightning, without an **E**, is bright flashes of light in the sky.

> The sky was **lightening**.
> forked **lightning**

loath, loathe
If you are **loath** to do something, you are very unwilling to do it.
To **loathe**, with an **E** at the end, is to hate something.

> I am **loath** to change it.
> I **loathe** ironing.

Remember: I loath**e** that **E** at the end!

lose, loose
Something **loose** is not firmly held or not close-fitting. To **lose** something is not to have it any more, and to **lose** is also to be beaten.

> *loose trousers*
> *Why do you **lose** your temper?*
> *We win away games and **lose** home games.*

mat, matt
A **mat** is a covering for a floor. A **matt** colour has a dull appearance.

> *the kitchen **mat***
> ***matt** paint*

metre, meter
A **meter**, ending in **ER**, is a device which measures and records something. A **metre**, ending in **RE**, is a metric unit of measurement.

> *the gas **meter***
> *ten **metres** long*

In American English, **meter** is the spelling for both meanings.

miner, minor, mynah
A **miner**, ending in **ER**, works in a mine. **Minor**, ending in **OR**, means 'less important' or 'less serious'. A **minor** is also someone under eighteen. Both of these spellings are also often used by mistake for **mynah**, which is the bird that can mimic sounds.

> *His grandfather was a **miner**.*
> *a **minor** incident*
> *a pet **mynah** bird*

morning, mourning

The **morning** is the first part of the day. **Mourning** is a form of the verb **mourn**, and means 'grieving for a dead person'.

> *morning coffee*
> *a period of* **mourning** *for the victims*

net, nett

A **net** is an object or fabric with holes in it. The **nett** result of something is the final result after everything has been taken into consideration.

> *a fishing* **net**
> **net** *curtains*
> *a* **nett** *profit*

of, off

Of is pronounced as if it ended with a **V** and is used in phrases like *a cup of tea* and *a friend of his*. **Off** is pronounced as it is spelt, and is the opposite of *on*.

> *a bunch* **of** *grapes*
> *They stepped* **off** *the plane.*
> *I turned the television* **off**.

palate, palette, pallet

The **palate** is the top of the inside of the mouth, and your **palate** is also your ability to judge the taste of food and wine. A **palette** is a plate on which an artist mixes colours, and a **palette** is also a range of colours. A **pallet** is a straw-filled bed, a blade used by potters, or a platform on which goods are stacked.

> *a coffee to please every* **palate**
> *a natural* **palette** *of earthy colours*
> *She lay on her* **pallet** *and pondered her fate.*

passed, past
Passed is the past tense of the verb **pass**. To go **past** something is to go beyond it. The **past** is the time before the present or describes things which existed before it.

> He had **passed** by the window.
> I drove **past** without stopping.
> the **past** few years

peace, piece
Peace is a state of calm and quiet. A **piece** is a part of something.

> I enjoy the **peace** of the woods.
> the missing **piece** of a jigsaw

> Remember: a **pie**ce of **pie**.

pedal, peddle
A **pedal** is a lever controlled with the foot, and to **pedal** something is to move its pedals. To **peddle** something is to sell it illegally.

> **pedalling** her bicycle to work
> **peddling** drugs

pendant, pendent
A **pendant** is something you wear around your neck. **Pendent** is a less common word meaning 'hanging'.

> a **pendant** with a five-pointed star
> **pendent** yellow flowers

peninsula, peninsular
Peninsula is the noun. **Peninsular** is the adjective.

> The Iberian **peninsula** consists of Spain and Portugal.
> a **peninsular** city

personal, personnel
Personal means 'belonging or relating to a person'. **Personnel** are the people employed to do a job.

> a **personal** bodyguard
> a change in **personnel**

pore, pour
If you **pore** over something, you study it carefully, and a **pore** is also a small hole in the surface of your skin. To **pour** something is to let it flow out of a container, and if something **pours** it flows.

> **poring** over a map
> The rain was **pouring** down.

practice, practise
Practice, ending in **CE**, is the noun. **Practise**, ending in **SE**, is the verb.

> target **practice**
> In **practice**, his idea won't work.
> We must **practise** what we preach.

> Remember that practi**ce** and practi**se** have the same endings as advi**ce** and advi**se**: **CE** for the noun, **SE** for the verb.

pray, prey
To **pray** means to say words to a god. An animal's **prey** is the thing it hunts and kills to eat.

> **praying** for a good harvest
> a lion in search of its **prey**

precede, proceed
Something which **precedes** another thing happens before it. If you **proceed** you start or continue to do something.

*This is explained in the **preceding** chapter.*
*young people who **proceed** to higher education*

prescribe, proscribe

To **prescribe** something is to recommend it. To **proscribe** something is to ban or forbid it.

> *The doctor will **prescribe** the right medicine.*
> *Two athletes were banned for taking **proscribed** drugs.*

principal, principle

Principal means 'main' or 'most important', and the **principal** of a school or college is the person in charge of it. A **principle** is a general rule, or a belief which you have about the way you should behave. **In principle** means 'in theory'.

> *The Festival has two **principal** themes.*
> *the basic **principles** of Marxism*
> *a woman of **principle***
> *The invitation had been accepted **in principle**.*

> Remember: My **pal** is the princip**al**; you must **le**arn the princip**le**s.

program, programme

A **program** is a set of instructions to a computer, and you can **program** a computer. A **programme** is a plan or schedule, and also something on television or radio.

> *a computer **program***
> *a **programme** about farming*

prophecy, prophesy

Prophecy, with a **C**, is the noun. **Prophesy**, with an **S**, is the verb.

> *I will never make another **prophecy**.*
> *I **prophesy** that Norway will win.*

quiet, quite
Quiet means 'not noisy'. **Quite** means 'fairly but not very'.

> *a **quiet** night in*
> *He is **quite** shy.*

> Remember: A qu**iet** p**et** can have qu**ite** a b**ite**.

rain, reign, rein
Rain is water falling from the clouds. To **reign** is to rule a country or be the most noticeable feature of a situation. **Reins** are straps which control a horse or child, and to **rein in** something is to keep it under control.

> *torrential **rain***
> *She **reigned** for just nine days.*
> *Peace **reigned** while Charlemagne lived.*
> *Keep a tight grip on the **reins**.*
> *She **reined** in her enthusiasm.*

rigor, rigour
Rigor occurs in the phrase *rigor mortis*, meaning 'the stiffening of a dead body'. **Rigour** is strictness or thoroughness, and **rigours** are difficult or demanding things about an activity.

> ***Rigor** mortis had set in.*
> *intellectual **rigour***
> *the **rigours** of the football season*

roll, role
A **roll** is something that is bent in a cylinder, and to **roll** something means to make it move like a ball. A **role** is the part that you play.

> *a **roll** of paper*
> *to **roll** the dice*
> *He played a major **role** in the incident.*

sceptic, septic

A **sceptic** is a person who expresses doubts. Something that is **septic** is infected by bacteria.

> a **sceptic** about religion
> The wound turned **septic**.

> Remember that these words are both spelt the way they are pronounced.

sight, site

Sight is the power to see, and a **sight** is something that you see. A **site** is a place with a special use.

> an operation to improve his **sight**
> I can't stand the **sight** of all this mess.
> a building **site**

stationary, stationery

Stationary, with an **A**, means 'not moving'. **Stationery**, with an **E**, is paper, pens, and other writing equipment.

> The traffic is **stationary**.
> the **stationery** cupboard

> Remember: Station**e**ry is **e**nvelopes, but station**a**ry is st**a**nding still.

stile, style

A **stile** is a step that helps you climb over a hedge or fence. **Style** is the way something is done, or an attractive way of doing things.

> He clambered over the **stile**.
> cooked in genuine Chinese **style**
> She dresses with such **style**.

---

storey, story

A **storey** is a level in a building. A **story** is a description of events.

> *a house with three **storeys***
> *a **story** my grandfather told me*

strait, straight

Strait means 'narrow', and is found in the words *straitjacket* and *strait-laced*. A **strait** is a narrow strip of water. **Straight** means 'not curved'.

> *the **Straits** of Gibraltar*
> *a **straight** line*

symbol, cymbal

A **symbol** is something that represents another thing. A **cymbal** is a musical instrument.

> *a **symbol** of fertility*
> *the clash of the **cymbals***

there, their, they're

Their is the spelling used to refer to something belonging or relating to people or things which have already been mentioned. **There** is the spelling for the word which says that something does or does not exist, draws attention to something, or says that something is at, in, or going to that place. **They're**, with an apostrophe, is a shortened form of *they are*.

> *people who bite **their** nails*
> ***There** is no life on Jupiter.*
> ***There**'s Kathleen!*
> *They didn't want me **there**.*
> ***They're** a good team.*

through, threw

Through means 'going from one side to the other'. **Threw** is the past tense of the verb *throw*.

*They walked **through** the dense undergrowth.*
*Youths **threw** stones at passing cars.*

tide, tied
The **tide** is change in sea level. **Tied** is the past tense of the verb *tie*.

> *high **tide***
> *a beautifully **tied** bow*

tire, tyre
To **tire** means to lose energy. A **tyre** is the rubber ring round the wheel of a vehicle.

> *We began to **tire** after a few miles.*
> *a flat **tyre***

In American English, **tire** is the spelling for both meanings.

two, to, too
Two is the number after one. The word **to** has many uses, such as indicating direction in phrases like *to the house* and forming the infinitive of the verb, as in *to go*. **Too** means 'in addition'.

> *I have **two** sisters.*
> *We went **to** Barcelona.*
> *I need **to** leave soon.*
> *Will you come **too**?*

tongs, tongue
Tongs are instruments for holding and picking up things. Your **tongue** is part of your body.

> *curling **tongs***
> *It burnt my **tongue**.*

vein, vain

Vain means unsuccessful. **Vain** also means proud of your looks or abilities. **Veins** are tubes in your body through which your blood flows. A **vein** is also a mood or style.

> a **vain** attempt to negotiate a truce
> You're so **vain**!
> the jugular **vein**
> writing in a jocular **vein**

> Remember: To be **va**in is **v**ery **a**rrogant, but a **ve**in is a blood **ve**ssel.

wander, wonder

To **wander** is to walk around in a casual way. To **wonder** is to speculate or enquire about something.

> She **wandered** aimlessly about the house.
> I **wonder** what happened

weather, whether

The **weather** is the conditions in the atmosphere. **Whether** is a word used to introduce an alternative.

> the **weather** forecast
> I'm not sure **whether** to stay or to go.

way, weigh

A **way** is a route or path, or a manner of doing something. To **weigh** something is to find out how heavy it is.

> Is this the **way** to the beach?
> You're doing it the wrong **way**.
> **Weigh** the flour.

which, witch
Which is a word used to introduce a question, or to refer to something or things that have already been mentioned. A **witch** is a woman with magical powers.

>*Which house is it?*
>*the ring which I had seen earlier*
>*a story about witches and wizards*

whose, who's
Who's, with an apostrophe, is a shortened form of *who is*. **Whose**, without an apostrophe and with an **E** at the end, is used when you are asking who something belongs to, or referring to something belonging or relating to things that have already been mentioned.

>*He knows who's boss.*
>*Who's there?*
>*a little boy whose nose grew every time he told a lie*
>*Whose coat is this?*

wrap, rap
To **wrap** something means to put something around it, and a **wrap** is something that is folded round something else. A **rap** is a sharp blow, and **rap** is a style of music.

>*to wrap presents*
>*a towelling wrap*
>*a rap on the door*
>*They like listening to rap.*

wring, ring

A **ring** is the sound made by a bell, and it is also a circle or enclosure.
To **wring** something is to twist it.

> the **ring** of the doorbell
> dancing in a **ring**
> **wringing** out the wet clothes

> Remember: You **w**ring out something **w**et.

wry, rye

Wry means 'mocking' or 'ironic'. **Rye** is a type of grass or grain.

> a **wry** smile
> a sandwich made with **rye** bread

yoke, yolk

A **yoke** is an oppressive force or burden. A **yoke** is also a wooden beam
put across two animals so that they can be worked as a team, and to
yoke things together is to link them. The yellow part of an egg is the
yolk.

> a country under the **yoke** of oppression
> They are **yoked** to the fortunes of the Prime Minister.
> I like the **yolk** to be runny.

your, you're

Your, without an apostrophe, is used when you are referring to
something belonging or relating to the person or people you are
speaking to, or relating to people in general. **You're**, with an
apostrophe and with an **E** at the end, is a shortened form of *you are*.

> **Your** sister is right.
> Cigarettes can damage **your** health.
> **You're** annoying me.

false friends

False friends

Knowing that words are related to each other can be a great help to spelling. For example, when you spell *typical*, it can help to think of the related word *type* so that you know that the letter after the **T** is a **Y**.

But there are a few traps. Sometimes it seems logical that a word should follow a certain pattern or be spelt the same way as a word that sounds like it, but you will find that it doesn't. You will need to be alert when you spell the words listed here.

aeroplane
> The beginning is **AE**. Don't be confused by *airport*.

agoraphobia
> There is an **O** after the **G**. Don't be confused by *agriculture*.

ancillary
> There is no **I** after the **LL**. Don't be confused by *auxiliary*.

bachelor
> There is no **T** before the **CH**. Don't be confused by *batch*.

comparison
> The letter after the **R** is an **I**. Don't be confused by *comparative*.

> Remember: There is no com**paris**on with **Paris**.

curiosity
> There is no **U** after the **O**. Don't be confused by *curious*.

denunciation
> There is no **O** before the **U**. Don't be confused by *denounce*.

deodorant
> There is no **U** before the **R**. Don't be confused by *odour*.

desperate
> The vowel after **P** is **E**. Don't be confused by *despair*.

develop
> There is no **E** on the end. Don't be confused by the ending of *envelope*.

disastrous
> There is no **E** after the **T**. Don't be confused by *disaster*.

duly

There is no **E** after the **U**. Don't be confused by *due*.

extrovert

The vowel before the **V** is **O**. Don't be confused by *extra*.

flamboyant

There is no **U** before the **O**. Don't be confused by *buoyant*.

forty

There is no **U** after the **O**. Don't be confused by *four*.

glamorous

There is no **U** after the first **O**. Don't be confused by *glamour*.

hindrance

There is no **E** after the **D**. Don't be confused by *hinder*.

hypochondriac

The vowel after the **P** is **O**. Don't be confused by the more common prefix *hyper-*.

inoculate

There is only one **N** after the **I**. Don't be confused by *innocuous*.

liquefy

The vowel before the **F** is **E**. Don't be confused by *liquid*.

minuscule

The vowel after the **N** is **U**. Don't be confused by *mini*.

negligent

The vowel after the **L** is **I**. Don't be confused by *neglect*.

ninth

There is no **E** before the **TH**. Don't be confused by *nine*.

obscene

There is a **C** after the **S**. Don't be confused by *obsess*.

offensive

There is an **S** after the **N**. Don't be confused by *offence*.

orthodox

The beginning is **OR**. Don't be confused by *authority*.

ostracize

The vowel in the middle is **A**. Don't be confused by *ostrich*.

personnel

There are two **N**'s. Don't be confused by *personal*.

pronunciation

There is no **O** before the **U**. Don't be confused by *pronounce*.

questionnaire

There are two **N**'s. Don't be confused by *millionaire*.

refrigerator

There is no **D** before the **G**. Don't be confused by *fridge*.

sacrilegious

There is an **I** before the **L** and an **E** after the **L**. Don't be confused by *religion*.

supersede

The ending is **SEDE**. Don't be confused by words like *recede* and *precede*.

truly

There is no **E** after the **U**. Don't be confused by *true*.

wondrous

There is no **E** after the **D**. Don't be confused by *wonder*.

other commonly misspelt words

Other commonly misspelt words

The final chapter of this book includes another list of words that are often spelt incorrectly. These words do not fall clearly under any of the categories covered in the previous five chapters.

Sometimes these words are hard to spell because the sound does not match the spelling. Sometimes the problem comes from the fact that a sound has several possible spellings and you need to know which applies in this particular word. Some of the words have several unusual features about them.

It is worth familiarizing yourself with these words. Helpful ways of remembering the spelling have been provided for some of them.

absence
There is a single **S** at the beginning and a single **C** at the end – just the same as in its opposite, *presence*.

abysmal
The vowel sound after the **B** is spelt with a **Y**.

accede
The ending is **CEDE** – just the same as in *concede* and *recede*.

ache
The consonant sound is spelt **CH** and there is an **E** at the end.

> Remember: An **ache** needs **a che**ap remedy.

acknowledge
The second syllable is spelt **KNOW**.

> Remember: The word is made from *ac + knowledge*.

adequate
The vowel after the **D** is an **E**.

advantageous
There is an **E** after the **G**.

advertisement
> There is an **E** after the **S**.

> Remember: The word is made up of *advertise* and the suffix *-ment*.

aerial
> The opening is **AE** – just the same as in *aeroplane*.

aesthetic
> In British spelling, there is an **A** before the **E**. The American spelling is *esthetic*.

aficionado
> The middle is **CIO**. The word comes from Spanish.

amethyst
> The second vowel is **E** and the final vowel is **Y**.

anaesthetic
> In British spelling, there is an **A** before the **E**. The American spelling is *anesthetic*.

analysis
> The vowel after the **L** is **Y** and the final vowel is **I**.

> Remember that *analysis* is related to *analyse*.

annihilate
> There are two **N**'s and the middle is **IHI** – just the same as in the related word *nihilism*.

anonymous
> The vowel between **N** and **M** is a **Y**, and the ending is **OUS**.

anxious
> There is an **I** after the **X**.

apology
> The vowel after the **L** is **O**.

> Remember: I will **log** an apo**log**y.

arbitrary
> There is an **AR** before the **Y** that is sometimes missed out in speech.

architect
> There is an **H** after the **C**.

argue
> The ending is **UE**.

atheist
> The first vowel is **A**, and the second vowel is **E**.

attendance
> The ending is **ANCE**.

> Remember: You **dance** atten**dance** on someone.

atrocious
> The ending is **CIOUS** – just the same as in *delicious*.

attach
> There is no **T** before the **CH** – just the same as in the opposite word, *detach*.

> Remember: Atta**ch** a **c**oat **h**ook to the wall.

auxiliary
> There is a single **L**, which is followed by an **I**.

awful
> There is no **E** after the **W**, and a single **L** at the end.

bachelor
> There is no **T** before the **CH**.

> Remember: Was **Bach** a **bach**elor?

barbecue
> The normal spelling is **CUE**. The word can also be spelt *barbeque*.

because
> The vowel sound after the **C** is spelt **AU**, and the ending is **SE**.

> Remember: **B**ig **e**lephants **c**an **a**lways **u**nderstand **s**mall **e**lephants.

beggar
The ending is **AR**.

> Remember: There is a beg**gar** in the ga**r**den.

berserk
There is an **R** before the **S** that is sometimes ignored in speech.

boundary
There is an **A** after the **D** that is sometimes missed out in speech.

breadth
The vowel sound is spelt **EA** and there is a **D** before the **TH**.

Britain
The final vowel is spelt **AI** – just the same as in *certain*.

> Remember: There is a lot of r**ain** in Brit**ain**.

broad
The vowel sound is spelt **OA**.

> Remember: **B-road**s can be quite **broad**.

bronchitis
There is an **H** after the **C**, and the ending is **ITIS**.

bruise
The ending is **UISE** – just the same as in *cruise*.

buoy
There is a **U** before the **O**.

> Remember: A **buoy** is a **b**ig **u**nsinkable **o**bject **y**oked in the sea.

buoyant
There is a **U** before the **O** – just the same as in *buoy*.

bureaucracy
The vowel in the middle is spelt **EAU** and the ending is **CY**.

> Remember that the start of this word is the same as the word *bureau*.

burglar
The ending is **AR**.
business
The opening is **BUSI**.

> Remember: It's none of your **busi**ness what **bus I** get!

caffeine
This is an exception to the rule 'I before **E** except after **C**'.
calendar
The vowel in the middle is **E** and the ending is **AR**.
carriage
There is an **I** before **AGE** – just the same as in *marriage*.
catalogue
The ending is **OGUE** – just the same as in *dialogue*.
category
The vowel after the **T** is an **E**.
cauliflower
The first vowel is spelt **AU**.
ceiling
The word begins with a **C** and the first vowel sound is spelt **EI**.

> Remember the rule: **I** before **E** *except after* **C**.

cellophane
The first letter is **C** and there is a **PH** in the middle.
cemetery
All of the vowels in this word are **E**'s.

> Remember: A parking **meter** at the ce**meter**y.

certain
> The final vowel is spelt **AI** – just the same as in *curtain*.

choir
> Nothing much in this word looks like it sounds: the beginning is **CH** and the vowel sound is spelt **OIR**.

> Remember: **Cho**irs sing **cho**ral music.

claustrophobia
> The first vowel sound is spelt **AU**, and there is an **O** before the **PH**.

cocoa
> The first vowel is **O** and the second vowel sound is spelt **OA**.

coconut
> There are two **O**'s – just the same as in *cocoa*.

coffee
> There is a double **F** and the ending is **EE** – just the same as in *toffee*.

competent
> The second and third vowels are both **E**.

> Remember: You must be **compete**nt in order to **compete**.

competition
> The vowel after the **P** is an **E**.

> Remember: You **compet**e in a **compet**ition.

complexion
> The letter after the **E** is **X**.

> Remember: **X** marks the spot!

concede
> The ending is **CEDE** – just the same as in *accede* and *recede*.

conference
> The vowel after the **F** is an **E** – just the same as in the related word *confer*.

congeal

The letter after the **N** is a **G**, and the ending is **EAL**.

conscience

The sound after the first **N** is spelt **SCI**.

> Remember: The ending is the same as the word *science*.

conscientious

The ending is **TIOUS**. The word is related to *conscience*, but the **C** changes to a **T**.

conscious

The sound after the first **N** is spelt **SCI**.

contemporary

There is an **AR** before the **Y** that is sometimes missed out in speech.

continent

The middle vowel is **I** and the ending is **ENT**.

controversial

The vowel after the first **R** is an **O**.

> Remember the related word *controversy*, where this vowel is sounded more clearly.

convenient

The ending is **ENT**.

counterfeit

The ending is **EIT** – just the same as in *forfeit* and *surfeit*.

courteous

The first vowel sound is spelt **OUR** and there is an **E** before the **OUS**.

criticize

The letter after the second **I** is **C** – just the same as in the related word *critic*.

crocodile

The middle vowel is an **O**.

> Remember: A cro**cod**ile has eaten a **cod**.

crucial
> The letter after the **U** is a **C**.

cruise
> The ending is **UISE** – just the same as in *bruise*.

currency
> The vowel in the middle is an **E**.

curtain
> The final vowel sound is spelt **AI** – just the same as in *certain*.

> Remember: Always buy pl**ain** curt**ain**s.

cycle, cylinder, cynic, cyst
> The opening is **CY**.

decrease
> The ending is **EASE**.

> Remember: Decr**ease** with **ease**.

definite
> The vowel after the **F** is an **I**, and the ending is **ITE** – just the same as in the related word *finite*.

deliberate
> The first vowel is **E**, and the ending is **ATE**.

> Remember the related word *deliberation*.

delicious
> The ending is **CIOUS** – just the same as in *atrocious*.

demeanour
> The ending is **OUR**.

> Remember: Demean**our** can mean **our** behavi**our**.

derogatory
> There is an **O** before the **RY** that is often missed out in speech.

> Remember: She was derog**atory** about **a Tory**.

describe
    The first vowel is **E**.
desperate
    The vowel after **P** is **E**.
detach
    There is no **T** before the **CH** – just the same as in the opposite word, *attach*.
deter
    The ending is **ER**.
different
    There is an **E** after the **F** that is sometimes missed out in speech.
dilapidated
    The beginning is **DI** (not **DE**).

Remember: A **di**lapidated building is **di**sused.

dinosaur
    The middle vowel is an **O**.

Remember: There are **no** di**no**saurs **no**w.

eccentric
    There are two **C**'s at the start.
ecstasy
    The ending is **ASY** – just the same as in *fantasy*.
elegant
    The vowel after the **L** is an **E**.

Remember: E**leg**ant **leg**s.

eighth
    There is only one **T**, even though the word comes from *eight + th*.

Remember: **E**dith **is g**oing **h**ome **t**o Henry.

either
> The **E** comes before the **I** – just the same as in the related word *neither*.

emphasis, emphasize
> The sound after the **M** is spelt **PH**.

encyclopedia, encyclopaedia
> This word can be spelt with either an **E** or an **AE** after the **P**.
> The vowel before the **P** is an **O**.

endeavour
> The middle vowel sound is spelt **EA** and the ending is **OUR**.

exasperate
> The beginning is **EXA** and the vowel after the **P** is an **E**.

exercise
> The beginning is **EXE** and the ending is **ISE**.

expense
> The ending is **SE** – using an **S** as in the related word *expensive*.

extension
> The ending is **SION**.

> Remember that this word is related to *extensive*.

extravagant
> The vowel after the **V** is an **A**.

> Remember: There are an extravagant number of **A**'s in extr**a**v**a**g**a**nt.

facetious
> The ending is **TIOUS**.

> Remember: The word fac**e**t**io**us contains the vowels **AEIOU** in order.

family
> There is an **I** after the **M** that is sometimes missed out in speech.

> Remember that you should be fam**i**liar with your fam**i**ly.

fascinate
    There is a **C** after the **S**.
fatigue
    The ending is **GUE**.
favourite
    The vowel sound in the middle is spelt **OU**.

> Remember: This one is **our** favourite.

feasible
    The first vowel sound is spelt **EA** and the ending is **IBLE**.
February
    There is an **R** after the **B** which is often missed out in speech.
feud
    The middle is spelt **EU**.

> Remember: **F**euds **e**nd **up** **d**isastrously.

fifth
    There is an **F** before the **TH**.
foreign
    The ending is **EIGN** – just the same as in *sovereign* and *reign*.
    This is an exception to the rule 'I before E except after C'.
forfeit
    The ending is **EIT** – just the same as in *counterfeit* and *surfeit*.
    This is an exception to the rule 'I before E except after C'.
friend
    There is an **I** before the **E**.

> Remember: **I** before **E**, except after **C**.

gauge
    There is a **U** after the **A**.

> Remember: **G**reat **A**unt **U**na **g**rows **e**ggplants.

generate, generation
> The vowel after the **N** is **E**.

genuine
> The ending is **INE**.

gipsy, gypsy
> The word can be spelt with either an **I** or a **Y** after the **G**.

glimpse
> There is a **P** after the **S** that is sometimes missed out in speech.

grammar
> The ending is **AR**.

> Remember that gramm**ar** is related to gramm**a**tical.

gruesome
> There is an **E** after the **U** and another at the end.

guarantee, guard, guess, guide, guillotine, guilty, guitar
> There is a **U** after the **G** in these words.

gymkhana, gymnasium
> The vowel sound after the **G** is spelt with a **Y**.

harangue
> The ending is **GUE** – just the same as in *tongue*.

hatred
> The final vowel is **E**.

hearse
> The vowel sound is spelt **EA** and there is an **E** on the end.

> Remember: I didn't **hear** the **hear**se.

height
> The middle is **EIGH** – just the same as in *weight*.

heir
> There is a silent **H** and the ending is **EIR**.

> Remember: **H**appy **E**dward **i**s **r**ich.

hereditary
There is an **A** before the **RY** that is sometimes missed out in speech.
holocaust
The vowel after the **L** is an **O**.
honorary
There is no **U** after the second **O**, and there is an **AR** before the **Y** that is sometimes missed out in speech.
horoscope
The vowel after the **R** is an **O**.
hyacinth
The vowel after the **H** is a **Y**, and the letter after **A** is a **C**.
hygiene
The first vowel sound is a **Y** and the second vowel sound is spelt **IE**.
hyphen
The first vowel sound is a **Y**.
hypochondriac
The letter after the **P** is **O** and this is followed by **CH**.
hypocrite
The letter after the **P** is **O** and the ending is **ITE**.
hypocrisy
The letter after the **P** is **O** and the ending is **ISY**.
hysteria
The first vowel sound is a **Y**.
idiosyncrasy
The vowel after the **D** is **I**, the vowel after the **S** is **Y**, and the ending is **ASY**.
imaginary
There is an **A** after the **N** that is sometimes missed out in speech.
incense
The letter after the first **N** is **C**, but the letter after the second **N** is **S**.
incident
The letter after the **N** is **C**, which is followed by an **I**.
incongruous
There is a **U** after the **R**.
independent
The final vowel is an **E**.

input

The opening is **IN**. This is an exception to the rule that the prefix **IN** changes to **IM** before a **P**.

integrate

The vowel before the **G** is **E** – just the same as in *integral*.

intrigue

The ending is **IGUE**.

introduce

The vowel before the **D** is **O**.

irascible

There is a **C** after the **S** and the ending is **IBLE**.

issue

There is a double **S** in the middle – just the same as in *tissue*.

itinerary

There is an **AR** before the **Y** that is sometimes missed out in speech.

jealous, jealousy

The first vowel sound is spelt **EA**; the second vowel is **OU** – just the same as in *zealous*.

jewellery

There is an **ER** before the **Y** that is sometimes missed out in speech. The American spelling is *jewelry*.

journey

The first vowel sound is spelt **OUR**.

Remember: How was y**our jour**ney?

judgment, judgement

There is an optional **E** before the **M**.

knowledge

The opening is **KNOW**.

Remember that **know**ledge is what you **know**.

knowledgeable

There is an **E** after the **G**.

labyrinth

The vowel sound after the **B** is a **Y**.

lackadaisical

There is a **CK** after the first **A** and the vowel sound after the **D** is spelt **AI**.

Remember: If you **lack a dai**ly paper you are **lackadai**sical

lacquer

There is **CQU** in the middle.

language

The **U** comes before the **A**, which is the opposite of the way the letters fall in *gauge*.

languor

The ending is **UOR** (not **OUR**).

laugh

The vowel sound is spelt **AU** and the final consonant sound is spelt **GH**.

league

The ending is **GUE**.

lecherous

There is no **T** before the **CH**.

leisure

The **E** comes before the **I**.

length

There is a **G** after the **N** that is sometimes missed out in speech.

liaise, liaison

There are two **I**'s in these words.

Remember: **L**ouise **i**s **a**lways **i**n **s**ome **o**ld **n**ightdress.

library

There is an **AR** before the **Y** that is sometimes missed out in speech.

litre

In British English the ending is **RE** – just the same as in *metre*. The American spelling is *liter*.

lustre
In British English the ending is **RE**. The American spelling is *luster*.

maintenance
The vowel after the **T** is an **E**.

mantelpiece
The letters after the **T** are **EL**.

margarine
The vowel after the **G** is an **A**. This is an exception to the rule that **G** is 'hard' before **A**, **O**, and **U**.

marriage
There is an **I** before **AGE** – just the same as in *carriage*.

massacre
There is a double **S** and the ending is **RE**.

> Remember: A **mass** of crops in every **acre**.

mathematics
There is an **E** after the **TH** that is sometimes missed out in speech.

> Remember: I teach **them** ma**them**atics.

meagre
In British English, the ending is **RE**. The American spelling is *meager*.

medicine
There is an **I** after the **D** that is sometimes missed out in speech.

messenger
The vowel after **SS** is **E** – just the same as in *passenger*.

minuscule
The vowel after the **N** is a **U**.

> Remember: This word is related to *minus*.

miscellaneous
There is a **C** after the **S** and a double **L**.

> Remember: Mis**cell**aneous **cell**s.

misogyny
  The ending is **GYNY**.
money
  The vowel after the **M** is **O**, and the ending is **EY**.
mongrel
  The vowel after the **M** is **O**.

Remember: A m**o**ngrel from M**o**ngolia.

monkey
  The vowel after the **M** is **O**, and the ending is **EY**.
mystery
  The vowel sound after the **M** is **Y**, and the ending is **ERY**.
mystify
  The vowel sound after the **M** is **Y** – just the same as in *mystery*.
nausea
  The vowel after the **S** is **E**.

Remember you might get nau**sea** at **sea**.

neither
  The **E** comes before the **I** – just the same as in the related word *either*.
neural, neurotic, neutral
  The opening is **NEU**.
niece
  The **I** comes before the **E**.
nuisance
  The opening is **NUI**.
onion
  The first letter is **O**.
ordinary
  There is an **A** after the **N** that is sometimes missed out in speech.
original
  The vowel after the **G** is an **I**.

Remember: I ori**gin**ally ordered **gin**.

ornament
   The vowel after the first **N** is an **A**.

oxygen
   The vowel after the **X** is a **Y** and the ending is **GEN** – just the same
   as in *hydrogen* and *nitrogen*.

pageant
   There is an **E** before the **A** which makes the **G** soft. There is no **D**
   before the **G**.

pamphlet
   There is a **PH** after the **M**.

parachute
   The ending is **CHUTE**.

paralyse
   The ending is **YSE** – just the same as in *analyse*.

particular
   There is an **AR** at the beginning and the end.

passenger
   The vowel after **SS** is **E** – just the same as in *messenger*.

peculiar
   The ending is **AR**.

penetrate
   The vowel after the **N** is **E**.

permanent
   The vowel after the **M** is an **A** and the vowel after the **N** is an **E**.

> Remember: A lion's **mane** is per**mane**nt.

persistent
   The ending is **ENT**.

persuade
   The beginning is **PER** and there is a **U** after the **S**.

phenomenon
   The middle part is **NOM** and the ending is **NON**.

pigeon
   There is an **E** before the **O** which makes the **G** soft. There is no **D**
   before the **G**.

pillar
There is a double **LL** and the ending is **AR**.
plagiarize
There is a **GI** in the middle.
plague
The ending is **GUE**.
pneumonia
There is a silent **P** at the start and the first vowel sound is spelt **EU**.

> Remember: **Pneu**monia **p**robably **n**ever **e**ases **up**.

poignant
The **G** comes before the **N**.
prayer
The ending is **AYER**.
prejudice
The letter after **PRE** is **J**.

> Remember: **Prej**udice is **prej**udging things.

prerogative
There is an **R** after the **P** that is sometimes missed out in speech.
prevalent
The vowel after the **V** is **A**.
primitive
The vowel after the **M** is **I**.
privilege
The vowel after the **V** is **I** and the vowel after the **L** is **E**.

> Remember: It is **vile** to have no pri**vile**ges.

protein
This is an exception to the rule 'I before E except after C'.
provocation
The vowel after the **V** is **O**.

> Remember that this word is related to *provoke*.

pursue

There is an **R** after the first **U**.

pyjamas

In British English, the first vowel is a **Y**. The American spelling is *pajamas*.

pyramid

The first vowel is a **Y**.

rancour

The ending is **OUR**.

recede

The ending is **CEDE** – just the same as in *accede* and *concede*.

rehearsal

The vowel sound in the middle is spelt **EAR**.

> Remember: I **hear** there is a re**hear**sal.

reign

The ending is **EIGN** – just the same as in *sovereign* and *foreign*.

relevant

The vowel after the **L** is an **E**, and the vowel after the **V** is **A**.

religion

There is an **I** before the **O** and no **D** before the **G**.

reminisce

The vowel after the **M** is an **I**, and the ending is **ISCE**.

rhythm

The beginning is **RH**, and the only vowel in this word is a **Y**.

> Remember: **R**hythm **h**elps **y**ou **t**o **h**ear **m**usic.

righteous

The ending is **EOUS**.

rogue

The ending is **OGUE** – just the same as in *vogue*.

sacrifice

The vowel after the **R** is **I**. The ending is **ICE**.

sacrilege

The vowel after the **L** is **E** – just the same as in *privilege*.

sausage

The first vowel sound is spelt **AU**, and this is followed by a single **S**.

sceptic

In British English, the opening is **SC**. The American spelling is *skeptic*.

schedule

The opening is **SCH**.

> Remember: The **sch**ool **sch**edule.

science, scientific

The opening is **SC**.

scissors

The opening is **SC** and there is a double **S** in the middle.

scythe

The opening is **SC**, the main vowel is **Y**, and there is an **E** at the end.

secondary

There is an **A** after the **D** that is sometimes missed out in speech.

secretary

The vowel before the **T** is **E**, and there is an **A** after the **T** that is sometimes missed out in speech.

> Remember: The **secret**ary can keep a **secret**.

seize

This is an exception to the rule 'I before E except after C'.

separate

The vowel after the **P** is **A**.

> Remember that this word has the word *par* contained inside it.

sergeant

The first vowel sound is spelt **ER**, and this is followed by **GE**.

series

The ending is **IES**.

serious
The ending is **OUS**.

several
There is an **E** after the **V** that is sometimes missed out in speech.

shoulder
There is a **U** after the **O**.

sieve
There is an **E** after the **I**, and another **E** at the end.

> Remember: A **sieve** is for **sif**ting **ever**ything.

similar
There is an **I** after the **M** that is sometimes missed out in speech, and the ending is **AR**.

simultaneous
There is an **E** after the **N**.

skeleton
The vowel after the **L** is **E**.

> Remember: Don't **let on** about the ske**leton** in the cupboard.

sombre
In British English the ending is **RE**. The American spelling is *somber*.

somersault
The first vowel is an **O**, and the final vowel sound is spelt **AU**.

soothe
There is an **E** at the end.

sovereign
The ending is **EIGN** – just the same as in *foreign* and *reign*.

> Remember: A sove**reign reign**s.

spontaneous
There is an **E** after the second **N**.

squalor
The ending is **OR** (not **OUR**).

stealth, stealthy

There is an **A** after the **E** – just the same as in *wealth* and *wealthy*.

stereo

The vowel after the **R** is an **E**.

> Remember: Ster**eo** **re**cords.

stomach

The first vowel is an **O**, and the ending is **ACH**.

strength

There is a **G** after the **N** that is sometimes missed out in speech.

supersede

The ending is **SEDE**. This word is not related to words such as *accede* and *concede* or *exceed* and *proceed*.

surfeit

The ending is **EIT** – just the same as in *counterfeit* and *forfeit*.

surgeon

There is an **E** between the **G** and the **O**.

> Remember: Surg**eo**ns give **e**ffective **o**perations.

surprise

There is an **R** before the **P**.

susceptible

There is a **C** after the second **S**. The ending is **IBLE**.

sustenance

The vowel after **T** is **E**.

synonym

There is a **Y** after the **S** and one before the **M**.

syringe

There is a **Y** after the **S**. The ending is **GE**.

tacit

The middle consonant is a **C**.

temperament, temperature

There is an **E** before the **R** that is sometimes missed out in speech.

> Remember that these words are related to *temper*.

temporary
   There is an **AR** before the **Y** that is sometimes missed out in speech.

theatre
   The first vowel sound is spelt **EA** and the end is **RE** in British English.
   The American spelling is *theater*.

thorough
   The final vowel sound is spelt **OUGH**.

through
   The vowel sound is spelt **OUGH**.

tissue
   There is a double **S** in the middle – just the same as in *issue*.

toffee
   There is a double **F** and the ending is **EE** – just the same as in *coffee*.

tongue
   The ending is **GUE** – just the same as in *harangue*.

tragedy
   There is no **D** before the **G**.

> Remember: I **raged** at the t**raged**y of it.

twelfth
   There is an **F** before the **TH** which is often missed out in speech.

typical
   The letter after **T** is a **Y** – just the same as in *type*.

usual
   The letter after the first **U** is **S**.

> Remember: **U**gly **s**wan **u**ses **a** lipstick.

vaccinate
   There is double **C** – just the same as in *access* and *accent*.

vague
   The ending is **AGUE**.

vegetable
   The vowel after the **G** is an **E**.

> Remember: **Get** some ve**get**ables inside you!

vehement

There is an **H** after the first **E** which is often missed out in speech.

vehicle

There is a silent **H** which is followed by an **I**.

veterinary

There is an **ER** after the **T** which is often missed out in speech.

vogue

The ending is **OGUE** – just the same as in *rogue*.

voluntary

There is an **A** after the **T** which is often missed out in speech.

vulnerable

There is an **L** before the **N** which is often missed out in speech.

weird

This is an exception to the rule 'I before E except after C'.

word

The vowel is sound spelt **OR**.

worship

The vowel is sound spelt **OR**.

wrath

There is a silent **W**, and the vowel is an **A**.

yacht

This is a very unusual spelling: the middle part of the word is **ACH**.

zealous

The first vowel sound is spelt **EA**; the second vowel is **OU** – just the same as in *jealous*.

Remember that this word is related to *zeal*.

index
of hard
words